MEETING IN FAITH

MEETING IN FAITH

*Twenty Years of Christian-Muslim
Conversations Sponsored
by the World Council of Churches*

Compiled by STUART E. BROWN

WCC Publications, Geneva

ISBN 2-8254-0949-9

Printed in Switzerland

Contents

III.   Regional Colloquia: 1983-1989

Introduction

Muslims and Christians have been in conversation ever since the dawn of Islam. Occasionally, their discussions took the form of systematic exchanges between limited numbers of persons with theological training and social or political standing; two famous examples are the interview between the Abbasi Khalifah al-Mahdi and the Chaldean patriarch Timothy I late in the eighth century C.E., and the audience granted to St Francis of Assisi by the Ayyubi Sultan al-Malik al-Kamil at Damietta in 1219. More often, Muslim and Christian rulers of varying degrees of piety incorporated religious differences into their economic and political rationales for intercommunal warfare, and scholarly studies of religion were nearly always designed to prove the truth of the author's position. A gradual and timid quest for another type of relationship has gained currency over the last century or so, leading to the Second Vatican Council's generous expression of respect for Muslims and other people of faith (1963) and the WCC's opening of a distinct section for dialogue in 1971.

At first, there was considerable uncertainty among the Christians about the methods or instruments which they ought to use in developing formal interfaith contacts. The WCC organized a series of meetings of Christians who were especially concerned with these questions, beginning at Broumana, Lebanon (June 1966) and culminating in the large consultation at Chiang Mai, Thailand (April 1977). Excerpts from the reports of six of these gatherings formed Part I of *Christians Meeting Muslims: WCC Papers on 10 Years of Christian-Muslim Dialogue* (Geneva, WCC, 1977), but the full text of the Chiang Mai report is still available and very current: *Guidelines on Dialogue with People of Living Faiths and Ideologies* (Geneva, WCC, 1979). It may be helpful simply to list the thirteen headings from these Guidelines to set the framework for the material at hand.

1. Churches should seek ways in which Christian communities can enter into dialogue with their neighbours of different faiths and ideologies.
2. Dialogue should normally be planned together.
3. Partners in dialogue should take stock of the religious, cultural and ideological diversity of their local situation.
4. Partners in dialogue should be free to "define themselves".
5. Dialogue should generate educational efforts in the community.
6. Dialogue is most vital when its participants actually share their lives together.
7. Dialogue should be pursued by sharing in common enterprises in community.
8. Partners in dialogue should be aware of their ideological commitments.
9. Partners in dialogue should be aware of cultural loyalties.
10. Dialogue will raise the question of sharing in celebrations, rituals, worship and meditation.
11. Dialogue should be planned and undertaken ecumenically, whenever possible.
12. Planning for dialogue will necessitate regional and local guidelines.
13. Dialogue can be helped by selective participation in world inter-religious meetings and organizations.

Virtually every one of these points has its echoes in the pages of this book, although no meeting yet has answered to all at once. A first set of six chapters offers the reports of the WCC's earliest endeavours at Christian-Muslim dialogue, from Cartigny, Switzerland, in March 1969 until the Nairobi Assembly 1975. Four of these were of a general nature, bringing together people of the two faiths from various regions of the world, but the last two were of regional focus (Africa, Asia).

Between the Nairobi and Vancouver Assemblies, there were another half dozen such meetings, and although most of these were of global dimensions; four were held in the environs of Geneva. Their reports form Part II of the present volume. The exchange on mission and da'wah (Chambésy, June 1976) has oft been cited as a lasting example of a sincere, constructive interfaith conversation, while the youth meeting at Bossey (June 1980) set a worthy precedent for interfaith encounters of young people in a variety of local situations. The smallest of these meetings may have been the most important, for it laid a foundation for institutional consultation that continues to develop (Cartigny, October 1976). Indeed, since 1986 representatives of the interfaith offices of the WCC and the Vatican have been meeting regularly with their counterparts from world Islamic organizations in a growing spirit of mutual trust and confidence; between these semi-annual sessions, contacts between these parties have become more frequent and cover an ever broader range of topics.

After the Vancouver Assembly, the swelling ranks of Muslims and Christians in all parts of the world who had an active interest in building constructive interfaith relations made possible the planning of a sequence of regional Muslim-Christian colloquia, and Part III comprises their reports. This group of meetings was designed to consider issues of local importance, to reinforce local interfaith communication and to contribute to the development of an international network of veterans of dialogue. This last objective will prove of special value in the near future as the WCC's section for dialogue seeks advice on the elaboration of a set of "ecumenical considerations" for Christian-Muslim dialogue. The matters discussed at the regional gatherings, the new trust which these meetings have fostered and the wealth of personal experience and perspectives gained by the participants all promise a rich harvest of mature reflection for this next phase in the work. (Reports from four of these colloquia are included here; the fifth is to be held in Arusha, Tanzania, in June 1989.)

This book, then, is both a documentary record of Christian-Muslim dialogue sponsored by the WCC and a corpus of basic texts for further exploration of the social, diaconal and theological frontiers of dialogue. It is a testimony to the growth of an idea and, finally, it is offered as encouragement and inspiration to all who would play a role in this happy adventure of understanding and peace.

STUART BROWN

The Beginnings
1969-1975

I. 1
Christian-Muslim Conversations

From 2 to 6 March 1969, at the invitation of the Faith and Order Commission of the World Council of Churches, twenty-two Muslims and Christians met together for four days of conversations in Cartigny, near Geneva. The foundations for this consultation had been laid by a smaller meeting in March, 1968, and this gathering represented an attempt to take up the developing interfaith conversation on an international level. The participants did not speak for the fellowships to which they belonged, but spoke exclusively in their own names. In the last two days of the meeting, the results of the discussion were brought together in the form of the following aide-mémoire.

1. Necessity of the dialogue

The participants of the meeting are agreed that the dialogue between Muslims and Christians is necessary, and that it should be established at various levels. This necessity arises out of several factors, e.g.:

a) the specific historical roots which the two religions have in common;
b) the attitude of self-criticism which is inherent in each religion;
c) the increased mobility and mixing of populations which has made meetings of Christians and Muslims much more common, and has increased the responsibility of the two religions to find ways of living together in the same society;
d) the special present situation, especially the common responsibility of both religions with regard to the political problems in the Near East.

The aim of the dialogue consists first in leading both religions to greater mutual respect and better understanding of each other. Their relations are

made difficult by a centuries-old history characterized by many misunderstandings. Further, the dialogue must aim to raise the questions which can
lead each of the religions to a deepening and a renewal of its spirituality.
Finally, such dialogue can lead to accepting and fulfilling common
practical responsibilities.

2. What do the two religions have in common?

Judaism, Christianity and Islam do not only belong together historically; they speak of the same God, Creator, Revealer and Judge. This fact
must be given expression in dialogue by using the same word for God.
The deep differences which exist must not be overlooked, however. They
are revealed by the very fact that the question of what is common in the
two religions is answered in different ways by Christians and Muslims.
Both religions have their own centre, from which they can be understood
in their wholeness. Examination of the other religion proceeds unavoidably from this centre. It is, therefore, understandable that what is
common is not formulated in the same way on both sides. What is
essential for the dialogue, however, is that common elements are seen on
both sides. The aim of the dialogue cannot consist in arriving at artificial
agreement. The encounter must not succumb to either syncretism or
relativism. Dialogue must open the way for the two religions, on the basis
of both their common ground and what is distinctive to each, to meet and
to ask each other the true questions.

3. Islam and Christianity face the questions of the modern world

The encounter of the two religions is taking place in a world which
finds itself in the midst of rapid change, in which the traditional religious
conceptions are being called into question. Islam and Christianity stand
before the task of formulating their belief in God in the present world,
and, above all, of living it in a convincing way. The dialogue contains a
special promise, if it does not confine itself to a comparison of traditional
positions, but rather turns to this task. The common roots can, in
discussion with the modern world, appear in a special way. This discussion includes such problems of social ethics as development, peace and
education. In particular, it must concern itself with the question of
knowing what serves the true liberation of man.

4. Intercourse between the religions

Meeting in dialogue presupposes that the adherents of each religion
conduct themselves in a new way to one another. Faithfulness to truth can

neither be disputed nor confined. Dialogue can be promising only when it recognizes this faithfulness. But it is necessary that this fidelity be expressed in a sympathetic understanding of the other religion. This signifies especially:

a) that one seeks to understand the other religion as it understands itself;
b) that one should always witness to the truth in respect for the other and for his freedom;
c) that every caricature not only be avoided but also struggled against;
d) that the conversation be carried forward in the expectation that one will learn both spiritually and intellectually from the other.

5. Tasks

The dialogue is only beginning. It must be expanded and deal with definite themes and questions, among which are the following:

a) How are Christianity and Islam being presented today in textbooks and religious instruction? What is the context of theological education?
b) What problems arise out of the fact that Muslim and Christian populations are mixing in ever-increasing numbers. How can these problems be solved?
c) How are we to think on the subjects of mission and proselytism?
d) Is there a possibility of common prayer between Christians and Muslims?
e) What responsibility do Islam and Christianity have in regard to the human and social problems of our time (nature and function of the modern state, emancipation of women, relationships between rich and poor nations, etc.)?

Such themes could be handled in broader international consultations. But dialogue on the local level is no less important. Study centres in different countries should be encouraged to concentrate on certain of these themes. For the continuation of the dialogue, a certain cooperation among the endeavours in the different countries is very desirable.

The participants in this consultation propose that a publication be planned in which recognized Christian and Muslim authors could express themselves. Such a volume would be intended to give a picture of contemporary Islam and Christianity in the spirit of this aide-mémoire. It could serve to widen the spirit of the encounter to larger circles.

I. 2
Dialogue between
People of Living Faiths

I

This consultation brought together three Hindus, four Buddhists, twenty-eight Christians (including five members of the staff of the World Council of Churches) and three Muslims. The participants came from seventeen different countries. They were invited by the World Council of Churches as private persons who were known to have experience of and concern for the development of positive contacts between people of different faiths. Many of them had carried out very considerable study of a faith other than their own.

The particular object of this consultation was to gather together the experience of bilateral conversations between Christians and people of the major faiths of Asia, with the full participation of members of these faiths, to experiment with a multilateral meeting and to see what could be learned for future relations between people of living faiths.

It was the experience of the consultation that something very new had been embarked upon. It was noted that this was the first time that people of these four faiths had been brought together under the auspices of the World Council of Churches. This, combined with the fact that the meeting was consultative and in no way representative, precluded the consultation from coming to any agreed statement of issues, let alone conclusions. Nevertheless, what was experienced together was felt to be very positive, a matter for general thankfulness and something to be carried forward urgently.

The keynote of the consultation was the understanding that a full and loyal commitment to one's own faith did not stand in the way of dialogue. On the contrary, it was our faith which was the very basis of, and driving force to, intensification of dialogue and a search for common action between members of different faiths in the various localities and situations in which they find themselves neighbours. This conviction was the presupposition of the consultation and was fully vindicated in a series of intensive and probing discussions which not only revealed many promising glimpses of agreements but also brought out and made clearer disagreements in understanding the world and man's place in the world. None the less the very disagreements were seen as points for further creative and intensive dialogue. Members were encouraged to discover how much careful attention and study had been given by members of one faith to the scriptures and tradition of another. Both the formal and private discussion and the opportunity to be present at and share in occasions of worship, prayer or meditation conducted by members of the various faiths contributed for further understanding not only at the level of concepts, but at the level of experience and devotion.

The consultation proceeded throughout in a sharp awareness of the pace of contemporary history and of the bitter crises in human relationships, nearest of all to us, that of this Middle East, because of our place of meeting. In all our "dialogical" exchanges, about this crisis as well as others, our remitting concern was with the question how to understand, and to translate into action and hope, what living commitment-in-faith requires of us, within the systems, the passions and the policies of which we are part.

The members of the consultation shared in an intensification of their sense of mutual concern for developing such dialogue in discussion, study and action and a common concern for the responsibility of all men of faith in and towards today's social and political problems. They were aware also of a personal sense of incompleteness and mutual need. It is hoped, therefore, that the initiative taken by the World Council of Churches in promoting multilateral conversations between men of living faiths will be continued and broadened, not only by the World Council of Churches but also, where possible, by appropriate initiatives from the side of the faiths other than the Christian. As explained above, the consultation was particularly concerned with Christians in dialogue with men of the main faiths of Asia. It was clear that a next stage would involve drawing people from other faiths and continents. The consultation was aware of the need to bring in members of the Jewish faith and of the religions of Africa at the next stage of dialogue. However, the whole enterprise has to be seen as at its very beginning, open to eventual participation by men of all faiths of the world as opportunities arise and situations permit.

In an attempt to convey something of what was entered into and enjoyed at the consultation and to exhibit something of so various, new, positive and yet tentative an experience, the consultation asked four of its members, one from each faith present, to write a brief personal reflection. These are given below as neither jointly representative nor jointly agreed but as presenting facets of our rich and promising experience. II is written by a Hindu, III by the Buddhists, IV by a Christian and V by a Muslim.

II

"At the very outset, I must confess to a sense of satisfaction of the kind that comes from participating in the happening of an event. The 'four-cornered' dialogue at this consultation marks the occurrence of a true happening. One is left with a feeling of having accomplished something, and it raises hopes of a preparation for continuing dialogue at future times. What are the factors that may have contributed to its success? The great organizational power and resources, and a certain theological sensitivity are, undoubtedly, among them, though they are reminders that the dialogue is organized under Christian auspices. Perhaps, without the theological 'axe', the consultation would have been little more than a vague gathering in pursuit of ill-defined objectives. The concern of the sponsoring body as to the outcome of the dialogue has been a major factor in steering the discussions in a creative direction even when the discussion tended to move on the 'debit' side.

"The most refreshing aspect of the consultation is the success with which a sense of recognition of the present historical context of religion, and of the historical responsibility of man today in the direction of dialogue could be wrested from the participants in spite of themselves, as it were. It is not the urge to confront and 'contain' the other as part of one's theological existence. It is not even the purely theoretic interest of dialogue for dialogue's sake with calculated indifference about its 'whither'. Dialogue is for the sake of man, to help recover his religious sense in the modern world vis-a-vis its anti-religious forces. To recover one's religious meaning is, among other things, to detect in oneself sources of irreligion, precisely in one's feeling of complacency and self-sufficiency about one's religious beliefs. Dialogue can be effective, as perhaps nothing else can, in helping one recover from being lost, religiously speaking, to the sense of self-assurance or adequacy and completeness.

"Our dialogue during these days brings home to us a new dimension of theologizing experience *viz* a felt sense of 'incompleteness', a sense of the need for the truly other — the 'other' in the way of thinking and feeling that I cannot simply assimilate to mine own, but which I confront inescapably, in other words 'encounter'. It is the 'other' which comes with the demand to be understood in terms of its incommunicable 'otherness'. This does not mean confessing to a theological deficiency in one's position. On the contrary, it speaks for the recognition of a new source of strength, hitherto remaining undetected. By virtue of its very adequacy and relevance, it opens itself for looking beyond itself, and evokes in one a creative need for the other.

"Interfaith dialogue is not a mere encounter of commitments and beliefs held in deep sincerity and faith, and acknowledgment and even promotion of the right of freedom of pursuit. While it is not less than this, it is certainly more than a meeting of faiths. It is 'sharing'. We had numerous exemplifications of this sharing in our dialogue. The idea and experience of 'suffering' God, of a sense of the divine that is with me not only in my joys but also in my sorrow, and, indeed, even in my unique experience as mortal *viz* death — this Christian experience could be shared existentially by a Muslim. This was reciprocated in a most spontaneous manner, and in the same existential strain, by a Christian who could commune with Islam in its uniqueness of 'letting God be God' as the name implied. He could feel the call for a 'sharing' of the total recognition of divine lordship itself understood as a system of monopoly. To the Hindu ears these ring a familiar bell, and more, he could feel the opening of a new dimension in the direction of greater specificity and concreteness in his religious existence. This is indeed a memorable experience.

"As a Hindu participant in the dialogue in depth during the two days of special sessions also, I could feel the effects of the creative impact of dialogue. It was creative not only in respect of the content of what I believe and feel. I felt enriched in that respect too. It was creative also in my understanding of what it is to believe primarily, confronting as I did ways of looking at issues foreign to my Hindu habit but at the same time compelling attention. I often felt reminded of the need on the one hand for increasing specificity and, on the other, for increasing relevance for actual life-situations today — 'how it cuts the edge of life at present, personally and socially' as one put it. 'On what spiritual grounds do the

Hindus engage themselves in their life-situations in the making of history', is a question that is going to haunt me for some time. In confronting this question, I not only become aware of the Christian presuppositions that underlie this business of making history, and of the more specific Protestant Christian slant of understanding religion in relation to secular-life-situations. I also feel the need for reassessing my Hindu premisses to be able to reach a conclusion that could meet the purely human requirement that stands underscored in the question.

"Our communion with men of other faiths is, prominently, a form of living our own faiths. To the Christian, it is living the 'witness' shown to him in the incarnation. To one who is not a Christian in the above sense, and who looks upon incarnation as an event given in Christian faith, it is likewise living the 'witness' of the light of his own faith. Dialogue between them should not only be possible but even fruitful for understanding man as man, and for understanding the deeper truth to which man bears witness which elevates him to spiritual freedom and to a vision of the spiritual presence in all the religious expressions of man."

III

"We Buddhists wish to place on record our sincere thanks to the World Council of Churches for the invitation extended to us. This, we believe, is a unique occasion for as we understand it it is for the first time in the history of the World Council of Churches that the Christians, Buddhists, Hindus and Muslims have met in dialogue.

"This consultation has, as it should, made us participants act in a spirit of cooperation rather than in a competitive way.

"Reflecting back on the dialogue itself, we are glad to state that we have been able to discuss freely ideas and concepts so divergently different to what we hold, in a very friendly atmosphere. But at the same time, we found that the semantic problem of terminology peculiar to each faith was a major factor that hindered a more fruitful dialogue. We also keenly felt that in the consultation, particularly in specialized group sessions, it was structured in a manner of one-way traffic in that our Christian brethren had the opportunity of knowing and sharing more about Buddhism and the opportunity afforded to the Buddhists to know about Christianity was not as much as we desired. We would have preferred had it been a two-way traffic.

"It is our conviction that as we all (Hindus, Buddhists, Christians and Muslims) each in our own way stand on strong and firm ground committed to our faiths, our dialogue in future should also be conducted with the same openness and frankness with a view to understanding each other's faith better, free from all bias, preconceived notions and prejudices. Such an attitude would lead us to more positive and concrete results as to our mission in future.

"It is also our candid opinion that dialogue should not be confined to mere academic level, but, if to be more meaningful, should take place at all levels of society. This dialogue, to us Buddhists, is a stepping stone to wider dialogue in the future.

"While maintaining the integrity of upholding the faith to which each one of us is committed we are of the opinion that dialogue can, and must, create and foster an atmosphere of tolerance and friendliness, wherein we can pool our common resources to work for the greater good of humanity.

"We Buddhists feel confident that dialogues of this nature will put an end to an era of anti-inter-religion and usher in an era of inter-religious cooperation so necessary in the modern context of religion and society.

"Above all, this dialogue has made us break away from our self-made barriers and paved the way to establish sincere friendship at the secular and spiritual levels between men of living faiths.

"If at the end of the consultation we have acquired nothing else, this last mentioned factor alone is ample reward we believe, in terms of the time, money and energy spent in convening a dialogue of this nature."

IV

"'Tell me your beautiful Names of God and I will tell you mine', said Munshi Zaka Ullah, a devout Muslim, to C.F. Andrews, Christian friend of India. We could be said to have been intending the same sentiment, in the intensive conversations of these nine days, as underneath our windows we have watched the Mediterranean, now scarcely lapping, now heavily pounding, the patient shore-line. We too have had our moods, within the undoubted community of heart we have experienced in the will to be 'penetrable' to one another. They can perhaps best be expressed in a number of interrogatives.

"Tell me and I will tell you... those beautiful Names... Is it all an exercise in mutual help to stay 'religious' in a world where no religion is any longer real? Are our pieties-in-converse essentially defensive, talking self-consciously of interior things because the harsh world is out of sight? Have we encased ourselves against its clamour, its economic and political disarray, its technological amalgam of assurance and anxiety, in what may become a seclusion of mutual patronage?

"What does it take to have it not so? We are of course only individuals. None of us, being counted easily on the fingers of the hand, even remotely represent the uncounted millions of our faiths. Even so, we are part of institutional self-interest. All our systems of thought are cultural 'empires'. Dialogue we find urgent as a repudiation of negativism and aggression. Yet are we truly in it, if we want it only for these 'defensive' reasons? The 'seriousness' of each faith forbids them to be closed entities, only capable of membership by accidents of birth and of geography. If they are impermeable to 'conversion', we have a situation quite intolerable to the dynamism of faith itself. Yet, given this necessary accessibility of each to all, how do we conceive our reciprocal duties? How do we relate these to our divergent doctrines? Can we see 'brothers' beyond the symbols of recognition normally required by our several faiths and liturgies? Are we, in part, already, what the other is in the 'part-truth' (if such we call it) of his 'insight' or his 'error'? If so, what is our proper relation, in thought and practice, to the becoming whole of that part-truth?

"May I, for example, see in Buddhist faith a profound psychological assessment of self-hood and its discipline, and reject it as a final ontology, for the sake of the 'psychology' itself? Am I right to embrace with reverent joy the categorical reality of Divine sovereignty in Islam, and yet yearn to find in it, for that very sovereignty's sake, the ultimacy of a love that suffers as my Christian faith bids me? What is my proper response if sincerity, speaking in other faiths, tells me: 'Truly we have Christ, but on our own terms'? Shall I then fear lest their terms reduce him? Do I still contend for the Christian terms, whose fullness I need if I am to have him truly? And if I so contend, am I caring about recognition for the Sonship which the New Testament tells me consists in *not* caring for itself, but in being 'emptied' for love's sake? Yet it is only a clear conviction, in doctrine, that Christ's is such a Sonship, which guards for me this truth that He 'takes the form of a servant'.

"It is in these and similar interrogatives that we best illustrate the converse we have had, in the discerning by each of the 'seriousness' of the other. It has been a heartening, if also sometimes bewildering, experience to have been at the water's edge of them.

"We have thought of what we should look for beyond these days. For my part our onward duties, mutual and separate, mean that we shall see faiths-in-relation as the deep test of faith itself. Whether we take it as paradox, or transcendental unity, or merely culture, the fact of our contrasts is the arena of our integrity.

"That test is set in the singleness and urgency of our contemporary humanity. We have to refuse the temptation to immunize faith from the tensions of the actual world. To think truly about God is to live pastorally among men, to live caring for the *Angst* of others as we learn it in the literature and the arts of our several cultures. For it is these who speak the silence of the inarticulate, as scholars, mystics or theologians rarely do.

"In gratitude for the opportunity we came together with convictions and uncertainties. We saw the way in and knew it as a duty. We do not yet see the way through. That both conviction and uncertainty have been confirmed can perhaps be taken as a sign of real hope. For integrity could hardly separate them. Some of us have a strenuous obligation of interpretation and of reassurance towards very many within our own tradition, who look with misgiving or perplexity upon our venture. It must be our yearning to hold fellowship inward when we seek it outward. The lengthening cords needs the strengthening stake. Or, perhaps in better metaphor, the donkey that precedes the eastern caravan is oddly cast without it!

"We are surely right in calling this only a beginning. But it would not be that, if we did not look eagerly for the sequel and expect it to be wider and deeper."

V

"The dialogue is a sign of hope, both for the inside and the outside of man.

"By the very fact that we lived together, over these nine days, shared our common religious concern, and also prayed together, we were made to feel something new, something which cannot be put into words except that we were all too small before God, too small to dispute him among ourselves, and that we had just to surrender, kneel down, and pray. This was the internal sign of the dialogue, what it did to us in our deep inside, and as its consequence many of us were led to feel that we were talking too much about God. This feeling tended to blunt the sharpness of our theological differences, and helped us to enter into a realm of ambiguity, as one participant remarked, which was creative on both the occasions when we prayed together, when we talked.

"Out of this creative ambiguity arose, as it were, an existential ambiguity linking us all in some deep sense of fellowship, intensifying on one side our respective identities as related to different religious backgrounds and on the other bringing them into a relation that was not experienced before. To most of us the 'other' faith was, before we actually met, an abstraction or just a different faith about which we knew less or more. But as we met, we became aware of a new situation, a kind of personal encounter, unfolding between us and within our common humanity which was, to translate it into religious terms, our common need of God. We felt, as we went through our conversations, that we needed one another, to help one another, to bring to each other the diverse modes in which God has spoken to man. This was the external sign of the dialogue which constituted both our differences and agreements.

"The dialogue, functioning as internal sign of hope, introduced most of us to a new spirituality, an interfaith spirituality, which I mostly felt in common prayer: who actually led the prayer or meditation, a Christian or a Muslim, or a Hindu, or a Buddhist, did not much matter, what actually was said during prayer was not all important, whether a Muslim would say 'Amen' after a Christian prayer mentioning Sonship of Christ was not the question; what we really became aware of was our common human situation before God and in God.

"We were thus led gradually into a new relation with God, with our own selves, and with others, and this new relation was perhaps to what the entire human history was moving, a relationship that was not new in the sense that it differed from what it was in each religious tradition but in the sense that it was expressing itself in a universal convergent humanity. A new day was dawning not on a new earth or in a new sky but on a new work of man, on man doing something new. This day is just begun. Our dialogue was therefore not an end but a beginning, only a step, and there is a long way to go. And there were dangers and temptations to take this sign of dialogue presumptuously, to immediately take it as a tool, as a means for remedying the given human situation in our century. It is a question of great care that a sign that points to a new relationship between God and man, man and man, should not be used as a social tool before the sign in question transforms our personality and matures us for its tests and challenges. We, however, feel great concern for the particular historical contexts and situations wherein men are living in hatred, suspicion, and distrust. But we are at the same time aware that 'dialogue' has to be 'lived' by each one of us in our particular social and religious environment to which we return after the consultation, and not to be merely advocated and propagated as an external tool. Let history be a challenge, not a master of dialogue.

"The feeling that dialogue is not the same in all interfaith situations was somehow brought home during the consultation. Though all religious traditions share the common ground of creative and existential ambiguity and of awareness of a common human situation before God and in God, it was however felt that the Christian, Muslim and the Jewish traditions have one origin, and perhaps share one common future. In the discussion on Christian-Muslim dialogue when the question arose of the ways in which the Christian needed the Muslim, and the Muslim needed the Christian, a great moment of convergence of feeling and warmth arose (perhaps it was the work of God) when it was pointed out by a Muslim that Islam, having started in history with all triumph and glory, needed, in order to grapple with the fact of the reversal of its historical fortunes, the Christian concept of suffering, a full sense of the tragic to transcend the limiting identity of faith and history. The response from a Christian, pointing how the Christian needed the Muslim, referred to the total sovereignty of God in Islam which could be of great inspiration to the Christian. Islam's notion 'Let God be God' could be brought to bear on the modern world which is vitiated by 'false absolutes'.

"It was this feeling of mutual enrichment and warmth that marked the specific group that met for the exploration of the particular issues involved in the Christian-Muslim dialogue. Even at the points of concepts of 'original sin' and 'salvation' where the Muslim and the Christian part ways, there was a serious effort to see any opening that could bring the concern of both to one common point of departure.

"The dialogue did undergo moments of tension, acute consciousness of theological and doctrinal differences, and awareness of ineffectivity and inauthenticity of dialogue carried in an insulated situation without relevance to the actual contexts from which the participants were drawn. There was a feeling of great inadequacy and tentiveness in spheres of discourse involving faith and history, and the challenge of modernity to all faiths. The dialogue was felt to be inadequate without reference to the actual areas and planes of conflict in the contemporary world. The actual and the symbolic value of dialogue both as a sign and as a means of reconciliation among men was felt to be brought into relationship with such concrete situations as the Palestinian issue in the Near East, the communal distrust and violence in India, the Buddhist-Christian tension in Ceylon, the Christian-Muslim encounter in Indonesia, etc.

"Out of several informal conversations and encounters among the participants a great feeling of belonging and sharing arose. What mattered most was not just dialogue but a special kind of community that the dialogue seemed to bring about. It was this sense of being drawn into a new community of men of faith that should operate in our particular social contexts. But this sense of being in a new community was not without inner threats and concomitant inadequacies.

"The first of them was the question of keeping one's own commitment to one's tradition undestroyed. I do not agree with the view that 'solidarity' of one's own commitment to tradition, community or church should remain wholly unmodified to make the dialogue authentic. One should accept that commitment to one's own tradition might expand into a wider loyalty to the common humanity within us all, and to the common feeling of God or Infinite. Secondly, the sense of being in a new fellowship might be inwardly thwarted by different and unequal concern for, and participation in, the historical processes of our time. When we enter into a new fellowship, we are not entering it as abstract entities or as historical units but as living persons with a great burden of both past and future. The new fellowship should thereby become an expression of the historical processes, and there are dangers of using it to further the very traditions which it is called upon to transcend.

"One of the great inadequacies of the consultation was that it only posed dialogue with the Christians on one side and each of the other three religions, say, the Christian-Muslim, the Christian-Hindu, and the Christian-Buddhist encounters particularly in the specific sessions. There could have been another structure, say the Hindu-Muslim, the Hindu-Buddhist, with other faiths as participants and observers.

"One of the most puzzling questions which I had put to myself, all the while during the consultation, was the relation between one's own cultural milieu and faith. We were in Ajaltoun all the time in a purely artificial situation, away from our respective cultural environments, not only in the sense of the general cultural milieu of our respective countries but in the sense that each of our faiths was related to a diverse and complex set of cultural and symbolic vehicles. This was exactly what I felt while attending two rituals in Beirut, one of Ashura, to which I belonged as a Shia Muslim, and another of service in a Greek Orthodox church. In the case of the former, it was a simple case of cultural alienation: though 'knowing' the significance and the religious import of Ashura and believing in it, I was not a part of its cultural and particular expression in the Beirut context. My own faith became an abstraction for me through the very feeling of cultural contrast in the modes of its expression. And in a very strange way the identity between faith and culture was both strengthened and broken down. I was exposed to the possibility of being irreligious and religious at one and the same time. The dangers and the obscurities involved in conceiving one's own faith in the universalist and abstract terms became clear. A dialogue taking place with less concern for the dynamics of tension between faith and culture was more an exercise in communication than an encounter of living men. Dialogue does many things to man. One of them is that it brings our hidden tensions and dichotomies into new relationships and perspectives. In the case of the service at the Greek Orthodox church, it was an experience of sharing in Christianity not as some abstract dogma, some system of belief to which Islam does not agree on certain particular and fundamental issues, but sharing in it within the media of symbolism and ritual. It is one thing to differ in abstract, and another thing to become aware of this difference in a symbolic medium. In the case of the former it is difference without feeling God's presence; in the latter case, it is a feeling of difference with God's presence all in and around. Hence, I tend to feel that dialogue through concepts is different from dialogue through symbols. The consultation was a beginning in the sense that it began with the intellectual encounter but it should lead to occasions of sharing each other's symbolic and cultural expression by living together in actual life-situations.

"It is in this sense that I take the community at Taizé in France as a light and a sign for all of us in future. It is by this living together and praying together that we understand much better the dichotomy of faith and history, of faith and culture, and also transcend it by the same means.

"We, in Beirut, have experienced a new opening, and wait upon God for his guidance and grace."

VI

The members of the consultation wish to keep in touch with each other, to widen the circle of reflection and to stimulate joint discussion on particular issues. They agreed that the results of the consultation should be communicated to the groups or organizations to which the participants belong and to the world organization of the different faiths.

In discussing further steps which might be taken to promote dialogue between men of living faiths, the following additional points were made:

1. Participants might help in promoting dialogues at local levels. Such dialogues might appropriately result in common consideration of social and political issues, and even joint action.

2. Further meetings of this kind might be planned. Future meetings should include members of other faiths, such as the Jewish faith, the African religions, etc. It was hoped that initiatives for some of these meetings might be taken by members of other faiths.

3. The implications of dialogue might also be considered in the educational field. The academic study of religions can contribute to preparation for dialogue and can itself be enriched by such experience.

a) Religious education syllabuses should provide facilities for sensitive teaching about different faiths.

b) Theological colleges and seminaries should develop provisions for the study of other faiths in the context of dialogue with adherents of other faiths (e.g. with visiting professors).

c) Educational institutions of one faith should provide pastoral care and religious instruction for students of other faiths in their own particular traditions.

d) Text books on religious education might be revised or written afresh, perhaps in collaboration with UNESCO, in order to ensure a proper presentation of the place of religions in the modern world and to avoid any caricature of one religion by the adherents of another.

4. There might be discussions between persons and agencies of those faiths which are also concerned with "mission". In particular, the issue of proselytism needs to be discussed together.

5. The following topics might be discussed at future meetings:

a) the meaning, basis and purpose of dialogue in relation to particular historical contexts;

b) dialogue and mission;

c) the process of secularization and the place of religions in relation to it;

d) the connection between spiritual experience, involvement in history and attitudes towards nature.

Participants

Prof. Masao Abe
362-Kamigoryo Banba-Cho
Kamigyo-ku, Kyoto, Japan

Prof. A. Mukti Ali
Institut Agama Islam Negri
Al Djami'ah Al Islamijah
Al Hukumijah
"Sunan Kalidjaga"
Jogjakarta, Indonesia

Dr W. Ananda Thera
International Buddhist Centre
International Buddhist Centre Road
Colombo 6, Sri Lanka

Father George Anawati, OP
Institut dominicain d'études orientales
1 rue Masna Al-Tarabich
Abbassiya, Cairo, Egypt

Dr Hasan Askari
Osmania University
24 University Campus
Hyderabad 7, India

Mr Sathira Bandharangshi
78 Indarabilaksa Road
Dhonburi, Thailand

Sister Lucienne Brousse
Soeurs Blanches — Centre d'Etudes
5 rue Abbé de l'Epée
Algers 3, Algeria

Mrs Margrethe B.J. Brown
COEMAR, 475 Riverside Drive
New York, NY 10027, USA

Dr John B. Carman
Center for the Study
of World Religions
Harvard University
42 Francis Avenue
Cambridge, MA 02138, USA

Bishop Kenneth Cragg
c/o Near East Christian Council
P.O.B. 5376
Beirut, Lebanon

Dr Kurt Dockhorn
Saarbrückener Strasse 169
33 Braunschweig-Lehndorf
Federal Republic of Germany

Dr Peter Doghramji
Near East School of Theology
P.O. Box 235
Beirut, Lebanon

Bishop Gregorius
Institute of Coptic Studies
Anba Rueiss Deir, Ramses Avenue
Abbassiya, Cairo, Egypt

Prof. C. Douglas Jay
Toronto School of Theology
4 St Thomas Street
Toronto 181, Canada

Metropolitan George Khodr
Archbishopric of Mount Lebanon
Hadath, Lebanon

Rev. Anker Gjerding
World Council of Churches
150 route de Ferney
1211 Geneva 20, Switzerland

Canon David Jenkins
World Council of Churches
150 route de Ferney
1211 Geneva 20, Switzerland

Father Klaus K. Klostermaier
Department of Religion
University of Manitoba
Winnipeg 19, Canada

Dr Peter D. Latuihamallo
Sekolah Tinggi Theologia
Proklamasi 27
Djakarta, Indonesia

Father Jesus Lopez-Gay, SJ
Ponteficia Università Gregoriana
Piazza della Pilotta 4
00187 Rome, Italy

Rev. Steven G. Mackie
World Council of Churches
150 route de Ferney
1211 Geneva 20, Switzerland

Venerable Ananda Mangala Thera
Thai Buddhist Temple
83 Silat Road, Singapore 3

Prof. Hans J. Margull
Jenischstrasse 29
2 Hamburg 52
Federal Republic of Germany

Father Vincent Miano
Secretariat for Non-Believers
Vatican City
Rome, Italy

Dr Nirmal Minz
Principal, Lutheran Theological
College
Ranchi, Bihar, India

Father Youakim Moubarac
Abbaye, 77 Jouarre
France

Swami Nityabodhananda
20 avenue Peschier
Geneva, Switzerland

Father Murray Rogers
Jyotiniketan, P.O. Kareli
District Bareilly, UP, India

Dr Hassan Saab
Fuad Soubra Building
Ibn Roshd Street, Al-Zaidania
Beirut, Lebanon

Dr S.J. Samartha
World Council of Churches
150 route de Ferney
1211 Geneva 20, Switzerland

Archimandrite Andre Scrima
Monastère Saint-Georges
Deir-El-Harf
Rass-El-Maten, Lebanon

Prof. Santosh Ch. Sengupta
Visva-Bharati University
Santiniketan
West Bengal, India

Rev. Lynn A. de Silva
The Study Centre
490 Havelock Road
Colombo 6, Sri Lanka

Dr K. Sivaraman
Birla Hostel
Banaras Hindu University
Varanasi-5, India

Mr Taika Sugai
The NCC Centre for the Study
of Japanese Religions
c/o Kyoto Diocesan Building
of the Japan Episcopal Church
Karasuma-Shimotachiuru-agaru
Kamykio-ku, Kyoto, Japan

Mr John B. Taylor
Selly Oak Colleges
Birmingham 29, England

Archimandrite Anastasios Yannoulatos
World Council of Churches
150 route de Ferney
1211 Geneva 20, Switzerland

Fr Christophe W. von Wachter
SODEPAX, 150 route de Ferney
1211 Geneva 20, Switzerland

I. 3
In Search of Understanding and Cooperation

MEMORANDUM

For a short but full week Muslims and Christians from twenty countries met together in Broumana, Lebanon. Some of us had met before and had already begun to share with each other the insights of our respective traditions. Nevertheless many were surprised by the friendly and trusting atmosphere of this conference.

We met as individuals, without any representative status; but we found our conversation, our meditations and our life together so significant that we feel bound to record our experiences. This memorandum is not a formal report and does not bind all participants. It has been discussed by the consultation but not voted upon. It is one way of confirming these experiences with each other, of sharing them with our own communities and of pledging ourselves and inviting others to further dialogue. This may be the dialogue of verbal colloquy, of shared work and leisure, or of a sense of common adoration of God.

1. What led us to meet?

In some measure we met because both past history and modernity have made it necessary for our two communities to encounter each other in many varying circumstances across the world. We work together in international and national development. We live together in the same localities and even in the same families. If we once confronted each other in hostility and sometimes failed to implement our own doctrines of religious freedom, our new feeling of interdependence makes it urgent that we seek new ways of dialogue.

For many of us there is a still more pressing reason why we should intensify deliberate efforts to meet each other. Beyond the sense of a common humanity and the inter-involvement of Christians and Muslims in history, there is a desire — belated for some of us — to honour together our conscious dependence upon God in a world that often seems to deny him. We wish together to obey God in the service of our fellow men and in the pursuit of justice and peace.

Some of us also wish to find a theological and, on occasion perhaps, a devotional framework for our mutual recognition and awareness. There is rich promise in our trying to bind together both the social and the spiritual ties which can unite us in a common basis. We know that we have sometimes widely differing political expectations and motivations, and sometimes widely differing theological language and doctrine between our respective traditions. Yet we have found that as we meet we can be renewed in our commitment to God and our fellow men.

2. Our hopes in the dialogue

We accepted that dialogue is not an attempt to supress differences but rather to explore them frankly and self-critically together with those who come from another tradition. Rather than being satisfied with a lowest common denominator, we faced up to sometimes poignant points of tension. Yet we also dared to hope for some convergence, not in impatient syncretism, but in openness to God's further guidance.

We hoped that we could shed all caricatures of each other's social and theological position. Our image of each other is often based on outmoded and by now reformulated positions. We wished to retrieve more positive evaluations of each other. While we saw that the same language or symbols could convey different meanings to our respective communities, we could hope to clarify how fundamental or how incidental these differences are. Such mutual discovery can lead us to a better awareness of what are the authentic issues for our dialogue.

In approaching these issues we accepted a clear individual responsibility. Whatever emerged as claimant upon us must be tested by us ourselves. We do not invite others to undertake something that some of us have not already tried or have not pledged ourselves to try. We dare to hope that such faithful experience may contribute not only to the renewal of our personal commitment to God but also to that of our respective communities.

We see that there is a challenge from the secular world to our religious communities that they should never again prove to be the instruments of mutual hatred and division in society. Only if we heed this may we, as religious men, challenge others to ask ultimate questions of life and death, of truth and goodness, of forgiveness and responsibility, of true community and suffering. For our dialogue is not only for our personal enrichment and for the enrichment of our mutual relationships. It is something which we wish to contribute to the world, and to offer to God.

3. Guiding principles for our dialogue

We do not desire to confine our conversation and our collaboration to a group of experts. We feel an obligation to help to make possible a wider spirit and practice of dialogue in our communities. We recognize that different situations call for different sensitivities, but that certain irreducible principles should be respected. The implications of these principles will be particular to various contexts and need to be patiently and practically worked out.

a) Frank witness: We did not ask each other to suppress or conceal his convictions. In dialogue each should bear witness of his motives to his fellows and to God. This frank witness can help to remove complacency, suspicion or unspoken fears.

b) Mutual respect: We believe that mutual respect was a necessary principle for our dialogue. This does not involve a stale coexistence of "live and let live", but a sensitive regard for the partner's scruples and convictions, a sympathy for his difficulties and an admiration for his achievements. We should avoid all invidious comparison of strength in our tradition with weakness in the other, of the ideal in one with the actuality in the other.

c) Religious freedom: We should be scrupulous about our protection of religious liberty. This involves not only the rights of any religious minority, but also the rights of each individual. While accepting that both religious traditions have a missionary vocation, proselytism should be avoided, whether by a majority intent upon pressing a minority to conform, or whether by a minority using economic or cultural inducements to swell its ranks. It is especially unworthy to exploit the vulnerability of the uneducated, the sick and the young.

4. What have we found in our meeting together?

Talking together with frankness and mutual respect, and aspiring to create conditions for full religious liberty and freedom of conscience, we have explored several major theological themes. Written papers and spoken contributions from members of both religious traditions have begun to show us a wider vision of world community, of our understanding of revelation, and of our role as religious men and women in many differing nation states.

We commend all these issues for further study. Ideally this should be undertaken in partnership between a Christian and a Muslim group or individual. We believe that theological and spiritual renewal can prepare us for social renewal.

a) World community: Muslims and Christians are called upon to achieve a wider vision of community, inter-racial, inter-cultural and international. This must often be tested and realized at the local level where religious pluralism provides a microcosm of the world's diversity. The quality of openness and cooperation in such local situations should make a vital contribution to the extension of inter-religious harmony and international justice.

We recognize the fact that it is desirable for a community to dedicate itself to the welfare of a local situation or nation. There may also be instances where a religious community must exercise its critical faculty over against a local political or socio-economic framework which is narrowly nationalistic, and hinders the establishment of world community, justice and human dignity. Christians and Muslims must actively contribute to redressing the wrongs of society, even at the expense of their own vested interests.

We expressed our very deep concern about many situations which are a threat to world peace and which create tensions among religious communities. We noted in particular the human tragedy of the Middle East and the many injustices against the people of Palestine, for which the world at large bears responsibility. We hoped that this crisis will be solved in the spirit of compassion and justice.

b) Revelation: In our attempt to be obedient to Truth our respective religious communities are wrestling with their understanding of revelation. We are aware of the suspicion and doubt of many modern men and of the rapidly decreasing impact of traditional language and symbolism. Within our religious traditions there is scope for reconsidering many of our theological and legal constructions; in this we should ensure continuity with the past, notably with our authoritative sources.

In our inter-religious study and colloquy we may find analogous as well as different understandings of revelation: for the Muslim the Qur'an is the word of God; for the Christian the Christian scriptures are a witness to the revelation in Jesus Christ. Our dialogue on such issues may help us to be more faithful to our own tradition as well as being more appreciative and more coherent with our neighbour.

Some of us felt that in further exploration of the experience of revelation in history and of God's guidance in our own lives we should be more open to the inexhaustible nature of the grace of God. We should also be more ready to bear a feeling of estrangement from our fellow men, even in our own tradition, as we strive, perhaps indeed on their behalf, to achieve a more critical self-awareness.

c) Religion and society: Dialogue does not take place outside a given political and socio-economic context. We deliberately avoided insisting upon a desideratum of a secular state or a religious state as being the more conducive setting for growth towards world community and obedience to divine revelation. The experience of our conference members was that social justice, spirituality and dialogue can and should be pursued in many differing political and cultural contexts.

Our involvement in society is part of our duty towards God. Some Muslims and Christians can speak of being co-workers with God in making history and in transforming society. We are aware of how we are confronted in new ways with the issue of religion in society. How far have our traditions failed our fellow men? How far do they hold new promise? We work together for self-critical re-evaluation of our roles and of our mutual relationships.

d) Our devotional practice: Our theological and our socio-economic concern need the spiritual basis and eschatological dimension of worship and prayer. Worship and prayer demand of us more than definitions, for they are the experiences of witnessing God and confronting the world. If our belief in the mercy and the justice of God impels us to work in the affairs of the world, how can Christians and Muslims relate their spiritual life to men's demands for justice, brotherhood and human dignity?

In the first place there is a constant requirement and hunger for each community separately to find spiritual nourishment in re-vitalized prayer and worship. The neglect of worship and prayer by many of our co-religionists is a challenge to us. The Muslim will be concerned to rediscover the fullness of *salat*, and the Christian to deepen the fellowship of the eucharist.

Where Muslims and Christians meet together we are not only listening to each other, but we are listening for God. On occasion, therefore, Christian and Muslim individuals or groups may also express their mutual understanding and trust in opening themselves to each other's devotional idiom, notably of *dua*, of supplication and meditation. Though conscious of our real and imagined differences in such actual or vicarious spiritual partnership, and though anxious to avoid misleading others, some of us felt that it was feasible to attempt this kind of interpenetration of mutual recognition and responsiveness to God.

5. What practical steps do we suggest?

We endorse again the variety of situations in which Muslims and Christians live, talk, think and work together. The dialogue may well carry political or social implications which must be consciously faced. Yet no local situation is completely immune from the possibility of its providing an inspiring example for men in other situations across the world, nor from the possibility of its learning from those others, nor yet from the possibility of its discouraging and embarrassing those others.

Accordingly we propose a catalogue of practical steps, some of which may be opportune in some situations, but not in others. Yet in our worldwide concerns and in our sense of worldwide community we desire to be alert to as many possible ways forward as there may be.

a) In our national and local communities: Christians and Muslims can and do cooperate with all their neighbours, as well as with each other, actively and prayerfully in nation-building, in ensuring human and religious rights, in struggling for justice and peace. They may work as colleagues in teams engaged in rural development, in literacy campaigns, or in medical clinics. They may together try to meet the problems of alienated youth through more patient response to their protest, and through providing counselling services or recreational facilities. Deliberate and self-conscious collaboration between Muslims and Christians, and with others, in such contexts may sometimes produce tensions, but it may also contribute to our mutual reconciliation.

b) Within our own religious communities: In working for the removal of our prejudices and for the furthering of a deeper mutual appreciation we reaffirm the urgency of avoiding all polemic, and of providing textbooks, teacher-training and seminary programmes which should be worked out in consultation with each other. We welcomed the emerging willingness for religious communities' gifts of material and practical aid to be channelled not through a particular religious community but given for the whole community, wherever the need is greatest. We regretted competition in building of places of worship and advocated closer social and spiritual contact between local congregations of the two traditions.

c) In further inter-religious dialogue: We determined to keep in touch with the results of local and international dialogues, and to work together not least on our own home situations in order to establish theological, missiological and societal principles for our dialogue and in order to find more opportunities for dialogue. By dialogue we understood not only meetings such as this, but also social collaboration, intellectual cross-fertilization, and, for some, vicarious participation in each other's devotional life.

We also took notice of our peculiar joint involvement in the traditional status of Jerusalem, the destiny of its people, and the historic significance of its religious and social character. On these spiritual and international problems, we aspired to the unity which that city should symbolize for all believers in God.

We are grateful for the initiative taken by the World Council of Churches, and hope that it will continue in its commitment to this dialogue. There is need to widen the basis of future dialogue, and therefore we look forward to initiatives by and coordination with various Christian and Muslim bodies.

Participants

Dr M.O.A. Abdul (M)
University of Ibadan
Department of Arabic and Islamic
Studies, Ibadan, Nigeria

Prof. A. Mukti Ali (M)
Minister of Religious Affairs
Government of Indonesia
Djakarta, Indonesia

Sheikh Mohammed Ali (M)
Bakwata, P.O. Box 21422
Dar es Salaam, Tanzania

Father George Anawati (C)
Directeur, Institut dominicain
d'études orientales
1 rue Masna al-Tarabich
Abbassiah, Cairo, Egypt

Dr Zafar Ishaq Ansari (Pakistan) (M)
College of Petroleum and Minerals
Dhahran, Saudi Arabia

Dr Hasan Askari (M)
Osmania University
Department of Sociology
24 University Campus
Hyderabad, India

Mrs Marie Assaad Abd El Moutagally
Assaad (C)
1095 Corniche El Nile
Garden City, Cairo, Egypt

Mr Mahmoud Ayoub (Lebanon) (M)
42 Francis Avenue
Cambridge, MA 02138, USA

Dr Zakaria Ahmad Mabrouk El Berri
(M)
Professor, Faculty of Law
Al Azhar University
Cairo, Egypt

Dr Samuel V. Bhajjan (C)
Director, Henry Martyn Institute
P.O. Box 153, St Luke's Compound
Station Road
Hyderabad 1, AP, India

Prof. Willem A. Bijlefeld
(Netherlands) (C)
The Hartford Seminary Foundation
55 Elizabeth Street
Hartford, CN 06105, USA

Dr Eugene C. Blake (USA) (C)
General Secretary
World Council of Churches
150 route de Ferney
1211 Geneva 20, Switzerland

Mr B.A.R. Braimah (M)
University of Ghana
Department for the Study of Religions
P.O. Box 66, Legon, Ghana

Dr Ali Dessouki (Egypt) (M)
Institute of Islamic Studies
McGill University
Montreal, Quebec, Canada

Father Michael Fitzgerald (UK) (C)
Pontifical Institute of Arabic Studies
49 Piazza Apollinare
00186 Rome, Italy

Dr Wadi Z. Haddad (Jordan) (C)
Associate Professor of Islamic Studies
The Hartford Seminary Foundation
55 Elizabeth Street
Hartford, CN 06105, USA

Dr Selim Haidar (M)
Shi'ite Higher Council
Hazmieh, near Bierut
Lebanon

Dr Mushir ul Haq (M)
Indian Institute of Advanced Study
Rashtrapati Nivas
Simla-5 HP, India

Dr Anwar Harjono (M)
Dean, Faculty of Law
Ibn Khaldun University
Djalan Marabahan 3
Djakarta 1/16, Indonesia

Dr S. Abid Husain (M)
Islam and the Modern Age Society
Jamia Nagar
New Delhi-25, India

Prof. Mahmoud Husain (M)
Vice-Chancellor
University of Karachi
Karachi-32, Pakistan

Prof. Yusuf Jaleel (C)
Gordon College
Rawalpindi, Pakistan

Metropolitan George Khodr (C)
Archbishopric of Mount Lebanon
Hadath, Beirut, Lebanon

Dr Peter D. Latuihamallo (C)
Sekolah Tinggi Theologia
Proklamasi 27
Djakarta, Indonesia

Dr Paul Löffler (West Germany) (C)
Near East School of Theology
P.O. Box 235, Beirut, Lebanon

Prof. Hans Jochen Margull (C)
Hamburg University
Sedanstrasse 19
2 Hamburg 13
Federal Republic of Germany

Mr Masudi (M)
Secretary to the Minister
of Religious Affairs
Department of Agama
Djl. M.H. Thamrin 6
Djakarta, Indonesia

Dr Bruce McLeod (C)
Bloor Street United Church
300 Bloor Street W.
Toronto 5, Canada

Dr Ali Merad (Algeria) (M)
Faculté des lettres et
sciences humaines
74 rue Pasteur
69 Lyon 7, France

Father Youakim Moubarac
(Lebanon) (C)
Abbaye, 77-Jouarre, France

Rev. Stephen O. Msangi (C)
ELCT Junior Seminary
P.O. Box 2
Soni, Tanzania

Dr Hisham Nishabi (M)
Makkassed Association
P.O. Box 5832
Beirut, Lebanon

Rev. Bolivar S. Ondo (C)
Aumônier du CEL
B.P. 41 Makak
Cameroun

Dr Muhammad Abdur Rabb
(Bangladesh) (M)
Department of Religion
Carleton University
Ottawa, Ontario, Canada

Dr Hassan Saab (M)
Fuad Soubra Building
Ibn Roshd Street
Al-Zaidania
Beirut, Lebanon

Imam Musa Sadre (M)
President of the Higher Council of the
Shi'ite Community
in the Lebanese Republic
Hazmieh, near Beirut, Lebanon

Dr Sheikh Sobhi El-Saleh (M)
Vice-President
Muslim Supreme Council
Professor, University of Lebanon
Beirut, Lebanon

Dr S.J. Samartha (India) (C)
Director, Programme on Dialogue with
People of Living Faiths and Ideologies
World Council of Churches
150 route de Ferney
1211 Geneva 20, Switzerland

Mr Lamin Sanneh (Gambia) (C)
School of Oriental and African Studies
University of London
Malet Street
London WC1E 7HP, England

Mr Muzammil H. Siddiqi (India) (M)
Center for the Study of
World Religions
Harvard University
Cambridge, MA 02138, USA

Dr Wilfred Cantwell Smith
(Canada) (C)
Professor of World Religions
Director, Center for the Study
of World Religions
Harvard University
Cambridge, MA 02138, USA

Dr R. Marston Speight (USA) (C)
30 avenue des Félibres
Tunis, Tunisia

Dr John B. Taylor (C)
Selly Oak Colleges
Birmingham B29 6LE
England

Dr Lukas Vischer (C)
Director, Commission on Faith
and Order
World Council of Churches
150 route de Ferney
1211 Geneva 20, Switzerland

Father Dr Y.A. Yousef (C)
4 Ahmed Hashmat Street
Zamalek, Cairo, Egypt

Dr Antonie Wessels (Netherlands) (C)
Near East School of Theology, Beirut
Institute for the Study of Religions
Free University of Amsterdam
P.O. Box 7424
Beirut, Lebanon

I. 4
Towards World Community

I. "Towards world community"

1. A multilateral dialogue

The bus moved past a Buddhist stupa, a Hindu temple, a Muslim mosque and a Christian church. A local committee consisting of members of these four communities was waiting to greet the fifty Hindu, Jewish, Buddhist, Christian and Muslim delegates arriving from over twenty countries to enjoy the stimulus and friendliness of meeting in Colombo, Sri Lanka, from 17 to 26 April 1974. The president of the Republic and local religious leaders associated themselves with this welcome to a multilateral dialogue organized by the World Council of Churches with consultants from all the five religious traditions involved.

As participants, many of us had taken part in previous bilateral or multilateral dialogues, whether organized by the World Council of Churches or by other bodies. We met in formal and group sessions under the guidance of chairmen drawn in turn from the respective traditions. We ate, relaxed or went sightseeing together. Each day began with an opportunity for those who wished to be together in silent meditation upon brief extracts of devotional and philosophical literature drawn from our various backgrounds. During a period of political unrest with a weekend curfew imposed we were constantly reminded of the world's social and economic condition. These factors together with religious and ideological criteria had appeared in many of the seven introductory papers, prepared by members of the five traditions and also by a nuclear physicist and a political scientist. We realized from these factors how urgent and also how difficult was the subject of our consultation.

Coming from widely different backgrounds, with differing self-understanding about our religious or ideological loyalties, none of us regarded himself or herself as an official spokesman for a particular religious tradition, ideological persuasion, age-group or interest-group. Nor did we attempt any combination of forces to exclude or criticize any group not represented. The experience of the meeting was itself, for many, sufficient justification for the conference. Yet there was also a constant intention to communicate to our own communities and to our other neighbours this experiment of common and also varying concerns for seeking world community. We hope that this memorandum will help not only to recapture for ourselves our own sense of quest and commitment but also to give encouragement in the many local or international situations where we, as well as other individuals and groups, are engaged in a dialogue of conversation and cooperation.

The wide spectrum of backgrounds and opinions in our group reflected some of the pluralism of our world and of many local situations. We acknowledged real polarities: in our views of history, perhaps linear, perhaps cyclical (perhaps not geometrical at all!); in our interpretations of the present historical situation in which we are living; in our desire or diffidence to conceptualize the ultimate; in our confidence or scepticism about the use of symbols or the place of devotions. We also acknowledged real common links, based on a sense of the universal interdependence and responsibility of each and every person with and for all other persons; we together recognized the fundamental unity of human beings as one family and committed ourselves to strive and, if necessary, to be ready to pay a price to realize the equality and dignity of all human beings.

We were conscious that we lived under a common threat of physical and moral and even spiritual destruction whether by warfare or starvation, whether by exploitation or enforced indoctrination. At certain points in all these areas we were conscious of compromise and lack of responsibility on our own part and on the part of our neighbours; but we also saw signs of hope where people were sharing or open to sharing their joys and their sufferings, their resources and their responsibilities. We saw such sharing as a hallmark of world community where hopes of goodwill, trust, peace and brotherhood might be fulfilled. Accordingly we set about envisaging the possibilities and potentialities of world community, conscious that our joint enterprise was bound to shatter some over-sanguine dreams and to challenge some over-cynical pessimism, but conscious too that our common search can be an act of faith.

2. *A provisional approach to "world community"*

Especially in the context of a world where so many of our fellows, young and old, find religious traditions disillusioning or distant, we find it hard to follow those religious or ideological leaders who promise easy panaceas. We question a utopian approach which oversimplifies the political, economic, cultural, environmental and many other problems involved. We look for a readiness for men and women from varying backgrounds and with varying motivations to accept each other's contributions. We have no illusions that some of us and some of our neighbours believe that our religions or ideologies make us arrogantly self-sufficient; we should beware of the danger of such self-sufficiency.

Each of us belongs simultaneously to different communities — religious, national and cultural — as well as to communities of common concern sometimes cutting across these lines. In striving towards world community we should attempt to achieve adjustment of these loyalties as well as try to learn to relate to members of other communities. Secular ideologies have addressed themselves to some of the same problems with which religions have tried to come to grips. We should therefore listen to their quests for solutions whether they are oriented towards national or social goals.

All of our religious traditions have emphasized mainly our responsibility to other human beings, whereas modern industrial society has put economic benefit and even a concept of "economic man" at the centre of its concerns. In some instances this self-centred view of the individual has been reinforced by religious institutions. In the attempt to create new forms of society there is scope for cooperation between religious people and those who derive their inspiration towards world community from other sources. Disagreements about fundamental issues and metaphysics should not necessarily mean that there is no scope for common endeavour on the level of social action.

A crucial factor in our deliberations has to be that on the level of physical resources one world already exists. Never in human history has the degree of interdependence and interpenetration of all human societies been so intensive. The energy crisis has brought this home to us all. This process makes every person into every person's neighbour, and the instruction to love one's neighbour, which is deeply embedded in various forms in all our traditions, cannot today be interpreted in a parochial way.

In facing the crisis of the future, there are five aspects that need to be examined more carefully.

a) the reordering of the relationship between the developed and the developing countries (radical and effective redistribution of power and resources including the reallocation of access to science and technology) while striving towards a new form of society;

b) the crisis of development within both developed and developing nations;

c) the phenomenon of violence in the struggle for liberation and social change;

d) the internal crisis in newly formed states — where people are grappling with the problems of nationalism, regionalism, linguistic exclusiveness and communalism;

e) the emergence of new models of society and their impact upon the fate and the role of religion.

If physical realities of economics and politics constitute evidence, then world community can already be observed in embryo. In view of this some of us are already anxious as to how existing or potential deformities may be avoided or overcome. We may also be challenged by a vision of how such a community could mature, in many forms and styles. Such a vision should not be a new and alternative social or spiritual absolute, but could give a spirit of unity in diversity, could challenge false absolutes, and could sustain those who choose or are forced into disengagement from existing structures which they see as unjust or blasphemous.

The fundamental assumptions behind science and technology as world-objectifying approaches to reality need to be examined. Some feel that the normal evolutionary development of the forces now operative in the world is more likely to lead to global catastrophe than to world community. According to them only a radically new approach to reality going beyond our present type of science and technology can hope to achieve a new pattern of human existence in which authentic and just world community could be achieved. It was thus recognized that any notion of world community would always be provisional. It must remain a transcendent ideal whose functional importance is proportional to its usefulness as a criterion for evaluation and as an orientation point for all human social achievements.

The diagnoses which we make for the divisions and the wrongs of our world may be different. Some of us point to the triumphalisms of our own or of others' cultural or political heritage as having undergirded commercial greed or doctrinal superiority; others of us may be concerned that a quietism has made us or our neighbours unduly weak. Some of us may urge the over-riding imperative of peace; others of us may urge a commitment to inavoidable conflict to achieve liberation. Despite these real tensions there is the common goal of world community, based on a readiness for responsible change and an openness to the future. A properly critical dialogue may expose these tensions without reconciling them but it may contribute to some mutual acceptance around the recognition of a common goal.

3. Structures towards world community

An attempt has been made to define or rather describe various clues as to the emergence of world community. We made appreciative reference to the many agencies of the United Nations, notably the Commission on Human Rights, despite our awareness of the disappointments and deficiencies that still exist. We took note that some of these agencies are still precluded (by what seemed to some of us anachronistic, culturally parochial constitutions) from dealing directly with most confessional or inter-religious bodies. The UN recognition of the World Conference on Religion and Peace was a hopeful sign. This initiative commands the respect of those of us who know of its concerns for situations of injustice, violence and want.

We may stand squarely behind the work of the United Nations especially in so far as it can transcend any restrictive definitions of national sovereignty and we may encourage responsible inter-religious organizations which do not minimize differences or disparage men's sense of identity in the interests of a universalist vision. We may also enjoy opportunities of exchange such as that afforded by the present multilateral dialogue. Nevertheless we saw that ugly forms of world community were also shaped by the armaments race, by the neo-colonialist debasement of aid into a tool for multinational commercial exploitation, by the religious or ideological manipulations of the weak by the strong, or by a triumphalist spirit in expanding world religious or ideological communities. Some of us took stock of how far we might be implicated albeit unwillingly in such manoeuvres or attitudes and we set ourselves to find more effective means of protest, rejection or reform, not least starting from the local level.

It was also at the local level that we saw some promising signs of fulfilling, in microcosm, the spirit of world community. This memorandum goes on to discuss and list resources and responsibilities for living together. It will be seen that it is the conviction of many of us that world community and living a life-in-community starts in the local situation within face-to-face relationships. From there it can expand to the regional and eventually to the national and worldwide context. It might be the special task of religious groups to stress the importance of models of concrete local community as the first reality of world community, but also as the reality which mediates the world community. At the local level each and all of us have opportunity to learn to accept and share with the people of different convictions in a spirit of mutual respect and reconciliation.

This does not preclude that local and even national communities should transcend themselves and learn to look at their situation in the perspective of world community. Our world has become one world and will stand together or perish together. This local and national community should have an open mind for the problems and tensions involved in the development of the world at large. At this point there is need to create a new spirit of openness amongst some political and some religious leaders or to have new leadership. Loyal to their own tradition and their quest for truth, these leaders could learn to make contact with and open their minds towards people of different convictions and towards the struggle of mankind for justice, and could inspire in their followers a similar concern.

The struggle for identity by some religious groups or nations may have made them unavoidably defensive and may have made them jealous of their hard-won sovereignty. Especially when religions provide an inspiration or a rationale for their group identity or nationhood it is also necessary to urge the claims of openness to other religions and ideologies and to a larger community of communities.

II. "Resources for living together"

In the newness of the world situation at the present time, we recognize the tension inherent in the differing, often diametrically opposed, demands made upon the resources of the individual communities. Such demands are made by the quest for a community of mankind on the one hand and for the preservation of particular existing and emerging societal forms on the other. We further recognize that while particular cultural, national, religious and ideological loyalties tend to assert themselves in the course of history, the nascent demand for world community which encompasses and transcends particular communities can only be brought into being by the concerted efforts of people striving towards its implementation.

In this task we must seek out in our respective traditions the resources which will further cooperation, the recognition of the equality of all men, their right to equal justice and to an equal share in material welfare. We must then seek to coordinate our particular efforts, based on the moral and spiritual values of religions, with other endeavours to achieve world community from whatever premise they arise, not to compete with them or to counteract them.

1. Obstacles to our search for world community

We are aware of the fact that this task entails a critical and self-critical assessment of our religious traditions, so as to bring into full light what in them is conducive to the achievement of community beyond the frame of the particular grouping, without minimizing the beliefs, doctrines and rites which establish the pecularity of each tradition. But before we come to claim these resources we must admit that there are many obstacles in our way. It is one of the tragedies of humanity that it can be precisely the striving for world community, expressing itself in various beliefs, which prevents the realization of this community here and now. A common way must be found while honouring the absolute claims of each concerning the world order.

We are fully conscious of elements in our traditions which because of their particularistic thrust have had a divisive impact in history, propelled men into mutual distrust, and generated hate and persecution. These elements block advance towards life-in-community in our own time. Some of these derive from the very matter of which our individual beliefs are constituted, others are generated by actual social, political life situations of religious men and religious communities. Even as we try to overcome such obstacles to community, every religion and ideology must be allowed to draw upon its own world community. In this context we found helpful the recognition of particularity as a universal empirical fact, and the affirmation of universality as our common goal.

2. Possibilities of finding common resources

Although we may not be able to conceptualize the common element, the experience of living together during these days has been an authentic expression of the already existing quest for resources for world community within all of us. We feel that enough resources exist in each religious tradition to strengthen this intuitive longing for world community. While respecting the peculiar sources that are valid for only one group or the other and which require to be spelled out in greater detail, we note with gratitude common elements in our religions that promote life-in-community.

a) Faith that our present human condition does not exhaust reality. (Human reality has a transcendental aspect expressed by some as a relationship with God and by others as a relationship with the Ultimate Truth; but we all consider that it is our right and duty not to submit to the human situation as it is but constantly to strive towards its betterment in history.)

b) The belief in the basic oneness of mankind, in the brotherhood of man, in humanity's destiny, in the responsibility of man to man, and in man as a transcendent reality.

c) The sense, of many, of the person in community as preceding the person as individual.

d) The conviction of the inherent inviolate dignity of the person, a dignity conditional neither on his or her adherence to specific convictions or doctrines nor on his or her sharing in specific insights or revelations.

e) The emphasis on loving-kindness and forgiveness.

f) The demand for dedication to the promotion of peace and of social and economic justice, for a struggle against social, economic, racial and religious discrimination. (Other people out of other secular or religious traditions may share these goals and may be called upon to share in this struggle against injustice and discrimination.)

g) Spiritual disciplines of worship and meditation to sustain human values.

3. The sharing of distinctive resources

As well as these more general resources to uphold and inspire the realization of world community, we gave careful consideration to the admittedly personal but nonetheless valid and original insights which the writers of our papers brought out of their respective religious traditions. Here it must suffice to quote some of their key ideas. A Muslim spoke of "a balanced synthesis of law and spirit"; a Jew explored "universality complementing particularity"; a Buddhist expounded "the Middle Path approach"; a Christian described an orientation "towards a communion of love" and a Hindu elucidated the idea of "tolerance as alternative absolutes". We also discussed the spiritual dimensions of the search for truth by scientists and people motivated by secular ideologies such as humanism, nationalism or Marxism.

Although no single concept of dogma or spirituality was fully accept-able to all five traditions we found areas of agreement between two or more traditions which need to be explored further in bilateral or multila-teral dialogue. For example, it would be useful to explore concepts like freedom, man, community, values, prayer, meditation, quality of life, essence and existence, and to see how different traditions accept or reject those concepts. One could also ask how far people from different traditions would agree to define spirituality in terms of disengagement from evil or unjust structures of society and of a search to create new forms of community embodying values such as selflessness, compassion, service to one's fellow men, simplicity and spontaneity, contentment and equanimity.

At one state in our discussions we had sought to find a framework or at least a set of categories with the aid of which we could discuss what is common in our five traditions. The issues of conceptualizing and sharing religious experience, realization, enlightenment, mystical experience and spirituality were examined and found to present difficulties. For some, however, who presuppose a personal awareness of these dimensions, these difficulties can be resolved by alternative modes of encounter beyond the intellectual and conceptual, although those same people are well aware of the danger of absolutizing their rejection of conceptualization.

We recognized the contribution of those mystics of all traditions who can transcend our conceptual distinctions and find common ground across the barriers of differing traditions. We were, however, not prepared to say that the conceptual divides, the mystical unites. The vast masses of religious people are still heavily reliant on conceptual structures whether or not they embark on the mystical quest. Not every religious person is prepared to make a choice between the conceptual and the mystical. We sensed that there is a range of distinctions, within which many nuances are preserved: there are, on the one hand, those traditions which affirm a personal God and would regard him as other than or beyond ourselves, and, on the other hand, those which seek the realization of Truth by being delivered from the illusion and the fetters arising from a false or deluded consciousness of self.

However, we agreed that spiritual values can be recognized in another person's religious tradition without necessarily adopting the language in which that tradition is expressed. The argument about means and ends may not be capable of resolution but there can be general agreement about the need to respect the other person's self-understanding and to accord him or her full freedom of religion. Even when inter-religious conversation does not lead to all-round agreement it can create mutual understanding and can promote harmony and concord among people of differing convictions. Dialogue must go on. It can be considered as a major resource towards world community.

4. Dialogue as one of the resources for world community

Dialogue involves the sharing of understanding and experience and as such is a significant method of building community. It is also a means of expanding self-knowledge and self-transcending knowledge. This implies more than a process of cognition. Dialogue can be a fundamental transforming process. We made six points about such dialogue:

a) It is a proper mode for discourse with one's neighbours.
b) It is a profound means of mutual understanding between individuals and between communities.
c) It is a preferable way of preventing clashes and settling conflicts.
d) It is a mode especially appropriate for spiritual and religious discourse.
e) It is a mode which is not confined to religious men and women but may be accepted by people who are motivated by secular ideologies.
f) It is sober, charitable and rational, and allows both critical and appreciative approaches.

By dialogue we understand a relationship and an interaction between people, not between belief systems. We see in dialogue a means of sensitizing people of various backgrounds to each other and through this to the common concerns of mankind. We do, however, feel that this quest for world community, while trying to transcend existing communities, need not weaken already existing communities, nor should it imply that one community is to be moulded in the image of another.

5. Yardsticks for religious and ideological resources

A final question remains about the viability and relevance of the resources claimed and offered in terms of the religious and/or ideological motivations of men and women in the modern world. By what criteria must these resources be selected; by what yardsticks must their fruits be judged? We looked for criteria and yardsticks concerning the influence of religious and ideological resources upon socio-economic conditions and upon the quality of life in a given nation or community of nations. We listed the following questions:

a) What contribution is made to community building — living and working together? How far is there a possibility of building up a morale that will inspire people to work, and to build up a national perspective with a wider vision?
b) What steps are taken towards the resolution of hostilities?
c) How far are science and technology and limited resources being shared more justly? How critically or uncritically are the fruits of science and technology appropriated?

d) How far is critical guidance given concerning implicit value judgments in planning and formulating policies of a country?

e) How far is the individual's conscience respected? How far are facilities available and freedom allowed to all for free exercise of their religion, for the communication of religious resources of different traditions and for the sharing of their experiences?

III. "Responsibilities for living together"

The notion of world community suggests the presence of a common link between all human beings. The link is, among other things, based on a new sense of universal responsibility, one that every person bears towards every other person. It is a responsibility that should express itself, not least at the local level, in a striving towards ensuring equal rights for all irrespective of religious and national differences. It should also express itself in an active concern for the other and an awareness of a common destiny.

1. The responsibility to overcome barriers

The responsibilities for living together require us to take due notice of those inbuilt elements in our religious traditions that hinder rather than help life in community, especially when the community in which we live assumes global proportions and becomes multi-religious in character. Ignorance about differing faiths and traditions gives rise to prejudices and mutual misrepresentations and caricatures. Even when better information is available from representatives of the respective traditions there is often a certain unwillingness to accept the integrity of adherents of those traditions.

Another closely related element that seems integral to our religious traditions and yet proves a major obstacle in the way of living together is the conviction of the ultimacy and finality of one's own religious tradition when it is so interpreted as to deny the authenticity of similar claims of finality on the part of other religions. There are two extremes, a dogmatism which in the name of ultimate commitment is insensitive to the reality of other faiths, and a syncretism which in the name of universalism undermines the religious identity itself. Both are hindrances to inter-religious community life.

Along with these is also to be listed proselytism, which can be a source of great disharmony between religions. The proselytizing efforts of a religion can seem unfriendly to the religious community to which they are directed; there can be an unethical way of employing in their service methods like the use of force, the giving of financial aid and the control of education. The misuse of such methods can be singularly unwholesome and create enduring sources of discord between religions.

2. A common commitment to reconstruct community

Our primary responsibility towards the task of living together as a world community is to seek for all a higher and a more just quality of life. This quest calls for an avoidance of those "blocks" that have for one reason or other been part of our religious traditions in the past, and for a reconstruction or rebuilding of our communities consistent with the new dimension that is introduced in our faiths, namely loyalty to the whole of mankind and not only to one component within it. Those elements in our traditions that promote life in community at large, emphasizing the inherent dignity of man, and his potential for sacrificing his individual interests for the welfare of all and for dedicating himself to the promotion of peace and of economic and social justice — these must be brought to the fore and strengthened.

The task of exploring and reinterpreting our religious traditions to meet the growing demands of world community implies our willingness to look at ourselves with critical eyes and our readiness to confront in our tradition anything that may, intentionally or otherwise, contribute to the demeaning of others. We should work for a diminution of that sort of influence so that the maximum contribution of love and human solidarity is secured. The task of "reinterpretation in integrity" is an internal task of each community of faith, in the fullness of its own authenticity, but the urgency and the awareness of this need is strengthened by dialogue and encounter with one another.

A sense of interdependence and mutual need, and a willingness to work together as one community encompassing the different communities of faith, are the imperatives that must be adopted to face the challenge of one world. This means removal of distrust and alienation and taking steps to work together under the conviction that inter-communal living is, inescapably, both necessary and desirable.

3. Ways of working together

Dialogue as a relation and interaction between people could become a means for promoting cooperation, mutual respect and tolerance for members of other communities. Dialogue offers to concerned people a method for working together to achieve practical goals. It can also be utilized in committees, conferences, informal get-togethers and interfaith discussions, focusing on concrete issues in society. Such encounters will enable us to bring together our various resources for dealing with the particular issues, and at the same time may sensitize people to new areas of human concern confronting us.

We hope that institutions could be established and movements among people encouraged on local, national and international levels to promote dialogue between people of different religious faiths. Such movements could work through informal groups or existing institutions, or through centres established for the purpose. Undue restrictions on travel must be removed in order to enable an effective continuance of the dialogue. Free movement between peoples, unhampered by political and other considerations, is an essential ingredient of world community.

We believe that men and women of goodwill should strive to create a strong public opinion in the world in order to bridge the existing gaps between the economic conditions of the people of developing countries. In this connection we take note of the possibilities, encouraged by religious precepts in some traditions, that loans granted by rich and developed nations and by some international agencies should be free of interest and of exploitative stipulations falling not least on future generations. We also assert that the developing nations have a right to a more equitable share in the natural resources of the world, and to have access to the technology and the availability of machinery of the developed and rich nations.

Among areas of common concern that need practical cultivation or implementation at the inter-community level are:

a) promotion of social justice within and beyond political borders;
b) common concern for environmental problems that span geographical and national boundaries;
c) promotion of a strong body of opinion across all religious communities against misuse of religion to justify prejudice or hatred or warfare but rather for the right use of religion to foster brotherhood and cooperation;
d) emphasis upon persuasive and peaceful means rather than violent and coercive means for the settlement of conflict;
e) education at many levels concerning different religious traditions, using authentic source books and jointly written or approved textbooks;
f) publication of, for example, journals for the promotion of dialogue and the exchange of ideas among scholars and leaders of religious opinion;

g) visits and exchanges between the teachers and the students of educational institutions which have a particular religious emphasis or constituency;

h) participation in cultural and recreational activities for all age groups in order to celebrate new experiences of community life which cut across religious and national lines;

i) respect for diverse forms of worship, meditation and prayer and more detailed consideration of the degree to which and the conditions under which reverent observation of each other's forms of worship and prayer may be undertaken;

j) for some, careful ventures into experience of common inter-religious supplication, meditation and intercession; this can lead to greater mutual understanding and can contribute to personal spiritual enrichment without involving any illegitimate syncretism;

k) the promotion of religious liberty and freedom of conscience for all parties; this involves mutual recognition and sensitivity in situations where some people feel a duty to give expression or bear witness to the faith by which they live;

l) support of inter-religious committees or movements dedicated to the establishment of goodwill, better community relationships, and the challenging of all forms of violence.

Finally, the group went on to make two recommendations, addressed initially to its own members:

We recommend that projects of human welfare on an inter-religious basis and with an inter-religious character should be supported. We were greatly enriched and stimulated by visits to the Prithipura Children's Home and the Sarvodaya Movement.[1] We agreed to study the feasibility of pilot projects, initiated or encouraged by members of this multilateral dialogue.

We recommend also that consideration be given to follow-up activities, drawing upon people from the various religious traditions represented at this meeting. We requested members of each community of faith to correspond with each other and with their co-religionists in order to prepare and to share a list of concerned people who might act as contacts

---

[1] The Prithipura Children's Home, Hendala, Wattala, Sri Lanka, is a combined effort of Christians, Buddhists, Muslims and Hindus to care for mentally retarded children in the context of a mutually supportive ashram and spiritual centre. The Home is associated with the inter-religious Asokapura community centre.

The Sarvodaya Movement is aimed at rural development on an inter-religious basis. Training programmes for young people and local self-help schemes are encouraged.

or resource persons to facilitate further dialogues. Together with such men and women, the participants might stimulate and coordinate the types of inter-religious cooperation itemized above.

* * *

We came to Colombo from the four corners of the globe with sometimes widely differing expectations. Our living together in community has strengthened in each of us the shared readiness to reach out beyond ourselves and our several traditions in the quest for a meaningful encounter with people of living faiths and ideologies. It has helped us to compare, criticize and correlate our visions of that aspired world community which was the subject of our deliberations. We leave our meeting grateful for the hospitality we have received in Sri Lanka and for a deepened sense of human fellowship, so necessary today not only for human welfare but also for human survival.

Participants

Hindus

Dr (Mrs) Sobharani Basu
Reader in Comparative Religion
Centre of Advanced Study in
Philosophy
Benaras Hindu University
Varanasi 221005, UP, India

Swami Chidananda
Sivananda Ashram
Rishikesh PO, India

Mr K. Lakshmana Iyer
Director of Education
Ministry of Education
Colombo, Sri Lanka

Mr S. Kathiravelupillai
MP for Kopay
68 Crossette Lane, Chundikuli
Jaffna, Sri Lanka

Prof. A.K. Saran
Professor of Sociology
Jodhpur University
Jodhpur, India

Dr K. Sivaraman (India)
Department of Religious Sciences
Faculty of Social Sciences
McMaster University
Hamilton, Ontario, Canada

Dr K.R. Sundararajan
Department of Religious Studies
Punjabi University
Patiala 147002, Punjab, India

Dr (Miss) C. Parvathamma
Professor and Head
Department of Sociology
University of Mysore
Manasa Gangothri
Mysore City-6, Mysore, India

Buddhists

Dr W. Ananda Thera
Head, Department of Buddhist Studies
(Sri Lanka University Kelaniya
Campus)
International Buddhist Centre
International Buddhist Centre Road
Colombo 6, Sri Lanka

Venerable Thich Nhat Hanh (Vietnam)
Buddhist Peace Delegation
69 boulevard Desgranges
F-92330 Sceaux, France

Prof. L.G. Hewage
Middle Path International
28 First Lane
Colombo 5, Sri Lanka

Venerable Ananda Mangala Thera
Chaplain, University of Singapore
Buddhist Society
Religious Adviser, Singapore
Polytechnic
Buddhist Society
122 Grange Road
Singapore 10

Dr Padmasiri de Silva
Department of Philosophy
University of Sri Lanka
Peredeniya Campus
Peredeniya, Sri Lanka

Venerable Dr H. Ratanasara
University of Sri Lanka
Vidyalankara Campus
Kelaniya, Sri Lanka

Mr Sulak Sivaraksa
Suksit Siam, Samyam Circle
1715 Rama IV Road
Bangkok, Thailand

Miss Nanda Leong Mei Yoke
Undergraduate, University of
Singapore, 718 D, Block 92
Commonwealth Drive
Singapore 3

Jews

Prof. Shlomo Avineri
Department of Political Science
Hebrew University
Jerusalem, Israel

Prof. Z.W. Falk
Faculty of Law, Hebrew University
Jerusalem, Israel

Prof. Irving Greenberg
Department of Jewish Studies
City College
140 Street and Convent Avenue
New York, NY 10031, USA

Prof. Shemaryahu Talmon
Department of Bible Studies
Hebrew University
Jerusalem, Israel

Christians

Prof. Bishop Anastasios (Yannoulatos)
of Androussa
University of Athens
14 Ioan. Gennadiou Street
Athens 140, Greece

Dr (Mrs) Margrethe B.J. Brown
128 Chaucer Court
Worthington, OH 43085, USA

Dr John M. Francis
Church of Scotland Home Board
121 George Street
Edinburgh EH2 4YN, Scotland

Prof. Douglas Jay
Director, Toronto School of Theology
4 St Thomas Street
Toronto 181, Ont., Canada

Prof. Hans Jochen Margull
Jenischstrasse 29
2 Hamburg 52
Federal Republic of Germany

Prof. D.C. Mulder
Jacob Marissstraat 108
Amsterdam, Netherlands

Mr Pontas Nasution
Director
Institute Oikumene Indonesia, DGI
Jalan Salemba Raya 10
Jakarta, Indonesia

Fr Prof. Daniel J. O'Hanlon, SJ
Jesuit School of Theology at Berkeley
Graduate Theological Union
1734 Le Roy
Berkeley, CA 94709, USA

Fr Dr Aloysius Pieris
31 Clifford Place
Colombo 4, Sri Lanka

Fr Murray Rogers
Jyotiniketan, POB 1248
Jerusalem, Israel

Dr Lamin Sanneh (Gambia)
Institute of African Studies
Fourah Bay College
Freetown, Sierra Leone

Dr Lynn A. de Silva
The Study Centre
490/5 Havelock Road
Colombo 6, Sri Lanka

General T.B. Simatupang
Jalan Diponegoro, 55
Jakarta, Indonesia

Dr M.A. Simandjuntak
Christian Conference of Asia
480 Lorong 2
Toa Payoh, Singapore 12

Father Joseph Spae, CICM
SODEPAX, 150 route de Ferney
1211 Geneva 20, Switzerland

Mr Robert L. Turnipseed
Ecumenical and International
Concerns Division
United Methodist Church
475 Riverside Drive, Room 1300
New York, NY 10027, USA

Fr Paul Verghese
The Orthodox Theological Seminary
Kottayam-1, Kerala, India

Muslims

Dr Zafar Ishaq Ansari (Pakistan)
Associate Professor of History
College of Petroleum and Minerals
Dhahran, Saudi Arabia

Prof. A. Mukti Ali
Minister of Religious Affairs
Government of Indonesia
Jakarta, Indonesia

Dr Hasan Askari
Osmania University
Department of Sociology
R33 University Quarters
Hyderabad 17, India

Mr B.A.R. Braimah
University of Ghana
Department for the Study of Religions
POB 66, Legon, Ghana

Dr Mushir-ul-Haq
Department of East Asian Studies
Aligarh Muslim University
Aligarh, UP, India

Mr M. Murad Jayah
95 Wekana Road
Colombo 2, Sri Lanka

Dr Mehdi Mohaghegh
Faculty of Literature and Humanities
University of Tehran
Tehran, Iran

Dr Hassan Saab
Professor at the Lebanese University
Fuad Soubra Building
Ibn Roshd Street, Al-Zaidania
Beirut, Lebanon

Dr Prof. Mohammed Talbi
University of Tunis
Les Palmiers, 11 rue de Téhéran
Le Bardo, Tunis, Tunisia

Drs A. Muin Umar
Lecturer of Islamic Studies
Institut Agama Islam Negeri
Jogjakarta, Indonesia

Staff

Dr S.J. Samartha
Director, Programme on Dialogue with
People of Living Faiths and Ideologies
World Council of Churches
150 route de Ferney
1211 Geneva 20, Switzerland

The Rev. Johan Snoek
Executive Secretary, Committee on the
Church and the Jewish People
World Council of Churches

Dr J.B. Taylor
Assistant Director, Programme on
Dialogue with People of
Living Faiths and Ideologies
World Council of Churches

Mr Michael de Vries
Secretary for Radio/TV Section
World Council of Churches

Mr Gilbert Cudré-Mauroux
Sound Technician
World Council of Churches

Miss Uta Hobrecht
Assistant, Programme on
Dialogue with People of
Living Faiths and Ideologies
World Council of Churches

Mrs Lynn de Silva
The Study Centre
490/5 Havelock Road
Colombo 6, Sri Lanka

Apologies

Hindus

Prof. K. Satchidananda Murty
Faculty of Arts, Andhra University
Waltair, Visakhapatnam 3, AP
India

Radhakrishna
Secretary, Gandhi Peace Foundation
223 Rouse Avenue
New Delhi 1, India

Swami Rangananathananda
Ramakrishna Mission
Belur Math
Calcutta, India

Buddhists

Prof. Masao Abe
362 Kamigoryo Banba-Cho
Kamigyo-ku, Kyoto, Japan

Dr Jothiya Dheerasekera
31 Palm Grove Avenue
Ratmalana, Sri Lanka

Venerable Dr Buddharakkhita Nayaka
Thera
Maha Bodhi Society
1st Main Road, Gandhi-Nagar
Bangalore, India

Rev. Terukastsu Okano
International Buddhist Exchange
Centre
Kodo Kyodan Buddhist Fellowship
38 Torigoe, Kanagawa-ku
Yokohama, Japan

Jews

Rabbi Louis Jacobs
38 Marlborough Hill
St John's Wood
London, England

Prof. Rabbi Norman Lamm
The Jewish Centre
131 West 86th Street
New York, NY 10024, USA

Prof. (Mrs) Chava Lazarus-Jaffe
Hebrew University
Jerusalem, Israel

Prof. R.J. Zwi Werblowski
Hebrew University
Jerusalem, Israel

Christians

Rev. Adeolu Adegbola
Institute of Church and Society
Box 4020
Ibadan, Nigeria

Miss Elisabeth Adler
Siemensstrasse 3
116 Berlin
German Democratic Republic

Miss Peggy Ashby
59 Croal Street
Stabroek, Georgetown
Guyana

Archpriest Nicolae Gundiaev
18/2 Ryleyev Street
Moscow 6-34, USSR

Metropolitan George Khodr
Archbishopric of Mount Lebanon
Hadath, Lebanon

Dr Peter Latuihamallo
Sekolah Tinggi Theologia
Proklamasi 27
Jakarta, Indonesia

Cardinal Sergio Pignedoli
Secretariat for Non-Christians
Vatican City
00193 Rome, Italy

Bishop J. Victor Samuel
113 Qasim Road
Multan, Pakistan

Dr David Stowe
United Church Board
for World Ministries
475 Riverside Drive
New York, NY 10027, USA

Muslims

Maulana Zafar Ahmed Ansari
12/8 Bunder Road
Karachi, Pakistan

Dr Ali E. Hillal Dessouki
Faculty of Economics and Political
Science, Cairo University
Cairo, Egypt

Dr Sirajul Haq
Department of Arabic and Islamic
Studies
University of Dacca
Dacca, Bangladesh

Dr Ali Merad
Faculté des lettres et sciences
humaines
74 rue Pasteur
69 Lyon 7, France

Mr Hisham Nashabi
Maqassed Islamic Association
Beirut, Lebanon

Prof. Dr S.H. Nasr
Shemiran, Amaniyah
Pahlavi Avenue
25 Farkhar Street
Tehran, Iran

Al-Haj S.M.A. Raschid
76 Manning Place
Colombo 6, Sri Lanka

Senator Mamintal Tamano
30 Behel Avenue
Quezon City, Philippines

I. 5
The Unity of God
and the Community of Mankind

The place and manner of our meeting
   Nine Muslims and eleven Christians from eight African countries met from 17 to 21 July 1974 at the University of Ghana, Legon, to explore ways in which African Muslims and African Christians can learn about and share in each other's religious traditions. Also present were several more Christians from Africa and other parts of the world, most of whom came in connection with the meeting of the Faith and Order Commission of the World Council of Churches. The WCC was one of the sponsors of the dialogue, which was co-sponsored by the Department for the Study of Religions of the University of Ghana and the Islam in Africa Project of the churches in Africa. A Muslim and a Christian were co-chairmen, and at the daily devotions an equal number of Muslims and Christians took turns in leading. At the invitation of local Muslims, a number of Christians attended the inaugural Friday congregational prayer at the new university mosque, and were also present at its official opening the next day. Muslims accepted a similar invitation to attend Christian worship on Sunday.
   Although Christians and Muslims had met each other elsewhere in the context of worldwide and local pluralistic situations, this was the first time they came together on an African regional basis. Our meeting has therefore to be seen against the background of such local-level and worldwide efforts. The underlying purpose of such meetings is the bringing together of concerned people from the major religious traditions as well as non-religious ideologies in a concerted effort to help provide a wider basis for human collaboration and action. Our Christian-Muslim

conversations are part of this ongoing concern, in which we envisage that not only religious people but others as well will be involved.

Common ground, concerns and responsibilities

Muslims and Christians in Africa, as in many other parts of the world, live in a pluralistic society where their status as religious people has provided the opportunity for personal contact at work and in society. Both groups, in their recognition and adoration of One God, share a monotheistic tradition. They also recognize many points of theological and spiritual convergence including reverence for Jesus. The adherents of both religions therefore have cause and ground for mutual recognition, respect and cooperation. They are particularly united in their common cherishing of the religious and moral values for which their respective traditions are distinguished. Furthermore, they are one in their common experience of the challenge with which materialism and modernism have faced religious and moral values. People of living faith from both sides ought to share their concerns and understanding, not in an attempt to forge an alliance against anyone but as a sign of their witness to God and of their responsibility for each other and the world.

In sharing together our understanding and experience of the world in which we live, we will be working together to try to build the world in accordance with the will of God as understood by our respective religious traditions. This can mean a common involvement in the concerns and interests of our African societies where religion is closely intertwined with social events. Our societies are fundamentally religious and have not made a rigid distinction between the sacred and secular. Our profession of God's sovereignty over all things and our duty to submit to him should be strengthened by a corresponding willingness to strive for mutual awareness and caring.

By sharing together our understandings, we should aim at trying to put into practice our mutual understanding. A greater degree of mutual sharing of resources should characterize our relations in society. For example, Christians should be willing to share with their Muslim neighbours those facilities and opportunities for religious, educational, social and economic advancement which Christians happen to possess. A similar spirit may be expected from the Muslim side. Such facilities should not be seen as power which one party tries to exploit in furtherance of its own domination over others. Rather, both sides should bear in mind the wider interests of the community under such circumstances. Both communities need to be particularly alert to the danger of assuming attitudes of superiority or haughtiness in those situations where, for whatever reasons, the resources of society are unevenly or even unfairly distributed among them. In those situations where immigrant members of one or the other religious community exist, we need to cultivate a spirit of hospitality towards them. As universal missionary-minded religions, both Islam and Christianity ought to show a particular regard for the strangers in our midst.

There is a great deal of concrete collaboration locally, especially with regard to the youth. In Nima, Accra, for example, a group of Ghanaian Christian students, in cooperation with Muslim students, is working together with some of the Christian population and a still larger number of Muslim inhabitants to help ameliorate people's physical needs. In that situation, local Muslims are acting as hosts. In one place where the church is well established, Christians have joined Muslims in demanding equal status for Islam and equal opportunities for Muslims. Another example is where a grant-aided Muslim secondary school has provided religious facilities for its majority Christian population. Examples are also known of places where a predominantly Muslim country has sponsored Christian schools, even though schools may be unwilling to provide religious facilities for the Muslim students going there.

The community and the individual

Already many African Christians and African Muslims live in the same community within which they meet together at home, work and service. Often they share the same experience of living in one community where they are linked not only by the same community obligations, but also by the intimate ties of family and friendship. Their sharing in community events involves them in each other's welfare, and this is poignantly emphasized when they meet at stress-points in life such as bereavements and funerals, disasters or emergency situations such as epidemics, famines, droughts and floods. Less dramatic but no less significant is the meeting which takes place on occasions of celebration like weddings, naming-ceremonies and reunions.

A natural meeting and sharing like that among ordinary people underlines the spirit of cooperation and mutual caring that goes far beyond the attitude that each religion must look after its own interests. It is against this background that the religious leaders of the two communities should come together and meet in a spirit of cooperation and sharing. Certain concrete steps can be taken. (1) Joint prayers can be offered for the welfare of the community as a whole. (2) Goodwill messages can be exchanged at religious feasts during the year, such as Ramadan, Id al-Fitr, Id al-Adha, Christmas, Easter and Harvest. For example, Christians could welcome a Muslim message at Ramadan which talks of the spirit of sacrifice and self-denial and urges the need for serving the interests of those with whom the community is shared. Similarly Muslims might appreciate a Christian message at Easter which expresses how suffering and sacrifice can be instruments of healing and reconciliation in the community. (3) Information exchanged about important events in each part of the community can further increase mutual trust and widen areas of credibility. National pastoral institutes, theological seminaries, National Christian Councils and their Muslim counterparts can work together in such areas as the following: (a) research into practical possibilities for collaborative schemes; (b) joint creation of centres for dialogue and informal meetings; (c) exchange of information about, and joint action in, situations of communal need; and (d) being active in conscientization and spreading interest in dialogue at various local levels so that it does not become, or appear to be, a specialist preserve.

Religious education and hospitality

Religious instruction in schools should not be limited to one community but must be provided for each religious community represented. Examples were given of Muslim schools which have provided facilities for the Christian pupils concerned, and of Christian schools where Muslim children were accorded similar facilities. However, there are other examples where one religious community has denied such facilities to the other and this practice needs to be seen as inconsistent, not only with the spirit of dialogue but also with the theological values of our respective traditions. Christian and Muslim schools should be open to the principle of providing teachers and educational materials for the respective religious communities. Even in schools and other institutions of education where only one religious tradition is represented, there is a strong case for instruction in both Islam and Christianity. In such instances, both groups need to be wary of the danger of manipulating educational power for a partisan cause. Each group should be open to the scrutiny of the other. Christian seminary training should include a course on Islam and opportunities for encounter with local Muslim representatives, and Muslim educational establishments should be similarly sensitive to the claims of their Christian neighbours.

Another matter which deserves the urgent consideration of both sides is the question of education and equal opportunity for women. Not only should religious education be offered equally to both sexes, but women should also have a share in controlling and carrying educational responsibilities. In some cases women have already realized a measure of equal status with men in this area. However, the question is now being more widely raised about increasing women's enrolment in religious institutions with the specific aim of having them fill religious offices in our communities.

Religious instruction should be concerned not only about teaching the established religious articles of our respective traditions, but also with the relationship between such instruction and the need for social change. A question was raised as to how a religion which sees itself or is seen to have been teaching values which are socially retarding, can still provide resources for changing those customs.

Family life and religious tolerance

In many places in Africa, Christians and Muslims live together as partners in the intimate closeness of marriage and family life. Sometimes a family under such circumstances is brought under pressure by the claim that the interests of one religion ought to prevail over the other. Mixed marriages, when placed under such particularly onerous demands, can lead to many kinds of family frustration and personal disenchantment. Far from prescribing a blue-print for the resolution of problems which people have to face on such a deeply personal level, we urge that individual families be encouraged to adopt whatever position they feel in conscience best suited to their need. It is a matter of widespread concern that religions should not attempt to impose conditions on people whose emotional involvement, of which marriage is the natural climax, makes them ready and prepared to cross religious barriers, particularly when such conditions pertain to children as yet unborn. Religious leaders should never try to exploit the emotional vulnerability of such people for their own narrow confessional interests, but must instead help these people to fulfill their potential and discover for themselves what is true for them. Where religious counsel is requested from one or the other religious tradition such help must be given, with the welfare and harmony of the people concerned as the over-riding consideration. It is unhealthy both for a normal family life and for the spirit of dialogue that religious competition should be extended into the field of family life and responsibility.

Medical ethics and religious propaganda

One of the most frequent areas in which people are thrown together as equals in spite of their religious affiliation is at the stress points of illness or disease. But what can be an occasion of mutual caring and active collaboration has sometimes been seized on as an opportunity for religious perversion and moral exploitation. A sick person, desperately in need of attention, has at times been looked upon as a prize to be won, for some religious cause. Sometimes a patient is required to submit himself to religious acts of worship of one or the other tradition of which he is not an adherent, as the price of medical treatment. Such exploitation of the weakness of others is a denial of the spirit of caring and selfless service which our religions enjoin upon us. While there is a place for seeking spiritual aid in the cure of physical maladies, there is no justification for applying our own religious criteria to people who may not demand it, consent to it or require it. Instead, religious services to sick people in medical and similar institutions, whether or not they be founded and run by religious organizations, should be given by the recognized representatives of the religious traditions concerned or with their authorization. Also, the training of medical personnel and the allocation of medical facilities should be undertaken on the basis of merit and need rather than privilege or favour. In medical work as well as in other areas of caring and service, religious people need to be scrupulous about the standards they apply to themselves so as to avoid the danger of their work and skills being misued or abused.

Dialogue

Dialogue grows out of these common concerns and out of an increasing awareness that we need each other for each other. It forms part of the realization that the way in which we recognize and adore God should be intimately connected with the way in which we cherish each other. The God of mercy and the God of love whom we honour and uphold is the same God we seek when we honour and uphold our common brotherhood.

Dialogue is therefore concerned about personal meeting and encounter and cooperation in work and worship, as well as about sustained mutual involvement in local level contacts. It can lead to a common desire for a search for truth and a reciprocal exchange of information and insights with each other, thus deepening and strengthening our knowledge of each other and of religious truth. This personal dimension needs to be stressed lest dialogue be mistakenly seen simply as some kind of comparative religion wherein academic comparisons are made of creed and dogma for their own sake. Also dialogue as the meeting of persons is different from, indeed critical of, conversion understood as a "numbers game" or a membership drive. That attitude, which sees conversion either as a piece of statistical manipulation or a triumphant band-waggoning, is contrary to the spirit of dialogue. Dialogue sees conversion as a growing mutual awareness of the presence of God in an encounter in which each becomes responsible for the other and where both seek openness in witness before God.

It is the ardent desire of participants in this dialogue that all our governments and religious communities will encourage the mutual support and tolerance which we have experienced here.

Participants

Muslims invited for dialogue

Dr Musa O.A. Abdul (co-chairman)
Department of Arabic and Islamic Studies
University of Ibadan
Ibadan, Nigeria

Mr Amadu-Suka
P.O. Box 3128
Accra, Ghana

Mr Ben-Yunusa
University of Ghana,
Legon Hall, F8
Legon, Ghana

Mr Abdullah Nasir Boateng
Ahmadiyya Secondary School
P.O. Box 3419
Kumasi, Ghana

Mr B.A.R. Braimah
University of Ghana
Department for the Study of Religions
P.O. Box 66
Legon, Ghana

Mrs Lami Futa
Hausa Section
Ghana Broadcasting Corporation
Accra, Ghana

Dr S.A. Kamali
University of Ghana
Dept. for the Study of Religions
P.O. Box 66, Legon, Ghana

Alhaji Mohammed Mahdi
28 Savage Square
Freetown, Sierra Leone

Mr Mustapha Talatu
Institute of African Studies
University of Ghana
Legon, Ghana

Christians invited for dialogue

Miss Mary Adoo
Operation Help Nima, P.O. Box 37
Nima, Accra, Ghana

Prof. Kwesi Dickson (co-chairman)
University of Ghana
Dept. for the Study of Religions
P.O. Box 66, Legon, Ghana

Dr Christian Gaba
University of Cape Coast
Cape Coast, Ghana

Fr J.R. Leferinck
National Pastoral Centre
P.O. Box 1989, Accra, Ghana

Mr Babs Mala
E 1/459 Labiran Street
Ibadan, Nigeria

Rev. Stephen Msangi
ELCT Junior Seminary
P.O. Box 2, Soni, Tanzania

Pastor Jacques Ndensi
Centre Liberté, B.P. 10027
Dakar, Senegal

Mr Kobina O. Odoom
Institute for African Studies
University of Ghana
P.O. Box 66, Legon, Ghana

Rev. E. Oyelade
Islam in Africa Project
Box 4045, Ibadan, Nigeria

Dr Lamin Sanneh
Institute of African Studies
Fourah Bay College
Freetown, Sierra Leone

Mr J.A. Sarpei
Secretary, Islam in Africa Project
P.O. Box 37
Nima, Accra, Ghana

*Faith and Order Commission
members, visitors and staff members*

Mr Martin Conway
Division of Ecumenical Affairs
British Council of Churches
10 Eaton Gate
London SW1W 9BT, England

Dr Karl-Christoph Epting
Hollerweg 8
785 Lörrach
Federal Republic of Germany

Dr Ellen Flesseman-van Leer
Netherlands Reformed Church
Amstelhoven 10
Amstelveen, Netherlands

Miss I. Friedberg
22 bis Chemin des Clochettes
1206 Geneva, Switzerland

Miss Marjory Havlick
B.P. 41
Makak, Cameroon

Mr Joshua Kudadjie
University of Ghana
Department for the Study of Religions
P.O. Box 66
Legon, Ghana

Bishop Francis Lodonu
Auxilliary Bishop of Keta
Volta Region, Ghana

Dr Geiko Müller-Fahrenholz
Executive Secretary
Programme on Faith and Order
World Council of Churches
150 route de Ferney
1211 Geneva 20, Switzerland

Rev. Jacques Ngally
Faculté de théologie protestante
B.P. 4011
Yaoundé, Cameroon

Mr Constantin Patelos
Secretary, Programme on
Faith and Witness
World Council of Churches

Rev. Jeanne Audrey Powers
475 Riverside Drive
New York, NY 10027, USA

Rev. Prof. V.C. Samuel
Orthodox Syrian Church of the East
Holy Trinity College
P.O. Box 30108
Addis Ababa, Ethiopia

Rev. Prof. H. Sawyerr
Fourah Bay College
Freetown, Sierra Leone

Mr Choan Seng Song
Associate Director
Programme on Faith and Order
World Council of Churches

Dr John B. Taylor
Assistant Director, Programme on
Dialogue with People
of Living Faiths and Ideologies
World Council of Churches

Dr Lukas Vischer
Director, Programme on
Faith and Order
World Council of Churches

Pastor Jean-Samuel Zoe
Faculté de théologie protestante
B.P. 4011
Yaoundé, Cameroon

I. 6
Muslims and Christians in Society

The place and manner of our meeting

Over 30 Muslims and Christians, in almost equal numbers, met in Hong Kong from 4 to 10 January 1975, to discuss the theme "Muslims and Christians in society: towards goodwill, consultation and working together in South-East Asia". They were made welcome in Hong Kong by local Christians and Muslims and worshipped there with their respective communities. The conference was organized by the department for Dialogue with People of Living Faiths and Ideologies of the World Council of Churches, Geneva, in cooperation with a committee of Muslims and Christians from South-East Asia and the Christian Conference of Asia. The joint chairmen were a Muslim, Senator Mamintal Tamano from the Philippines, and a Christian, Dr Peter Latuihamallo from Indonesia. Papers were prepared by Prof. Cesar Majul of the Philippines and Dr Ahmad Ibrahim of Malaysia, on the Muslim side. On the Christian side, Dr Ihromi of Indonesia, Sister Theresa Thong of Malaysia and Mrs Portia Mapanao of the Philippines introduced subjects which ranged from theological grounds for inter-religious respect to practical experience of the role of religion in promoting or disturbing social harmony.

This was the first time that such a regional conference had been held in South-East Asia, although several of the participants had attended international Christian-Muslim dialogues or have been active in their local situations in conversation and cooperation with their neighbours of another faith. The conference considered some guidelines which could further stimulate regional and local dialogues of this nature, not only in the interests of nation-building and community development but also in the interests of building up spiritual values and resources of goodwill, respect and faith in the face of common problems and opportunities in the modern world.

The participants expressed their joy in meeting together and they also hoped that such encounters might be repeated in the future. They together discussed the following memorandum which, without presuming to speak for any religious organization or community as a whole, nevertheless met with the careful and glad consensus of all those present who recommended it to their respective communities for further consultation and, where appropriate, implementation.

The need for Muslim-Christian dialogue in South-East Asia

It is a sad fact that, often in the past and even at the present time, attitudes of exclusivism, of condescension or of hostility have characterized relations between Muslims and Christians in South-East Asia. We Christians and Muslims, coming together in dialogue in Hong Kong from different situations, whether of cooperation and harmony or of tension and conflict between our communities in South-East Asia, recognize that any negative attitudes do not reflect the true character of either of our faiths. Any such attitudes illustrate the gap which exists in both communities between the high principles of religious teaching and the actual practices of their adherents.

Our purpose in Hong Kong has been to face up to the fact that we come from religiously pluralistic societies in South-East Asia, wherein not only is conflict clearly disastrous but even peaceful co-existence is an inadequate condition for the urgent needs of our developing societies. Our respective national societies, we feel, have a right to expect from the faithful communities of Christians and Muslims not conflict, not mere coexistence, but good-will, a readiness to confer with each other and an eagerness to cooperate in every possible way. Muslims and Christians need each other's help to ease tension, secure justice, relieve pain, and otherwise promote the social, material and spiritual wellbeing of all people.

The theological bases for Muslim-Christian relations and for the relations of both with all neighbouring religions and ideologies

We Christians and Muslims meeting in Hong Kong affirm that our respective faiths, properly understood, enjoin on us a loving relationship with each other and with all human beings. The ground and impetus for this living relationship is no less than the One God himself who has made all human beings brothers and sisters. Muslims emphasize that God the Compassionate (*Al-Rahmān*) and the Beloved (*Al-Habīb*) commands the faithful to be merciful and compassionate and loving in their dealings with all people, and therefore they are able to be so. The Qur'an embodies this command and specifies ways in which the faithful may obediently comply with it in various life situations. Christians, for their part, emphasize that God's love shown in his self-giving in and through the person of Jesus Christ both inspires and enables their loving relationship with all human-kind. Responding to God's love in Jesus Christ, Christians find the example and basis for love in their social dealings with all people. Thus, allowing for these differences in understanding, both Islam and Christianity find their ethical mandate in the All-Merciful God who loves and is loved.

We Christians and Muslims in South-East Asia are only too painfully aware of how far short we have fallen from God's will for us in our encounters with one another. We acknowledge together that individuals and groups from both communities have often forgotten that power — whether financial or political or social or cultural or intellectual or spiritual — is a trust (*amānah*) from God to be used responsibly and compassionately for the wellbeing of all, and not abused to advance the selfish interests of a particular individual or group or ideology.

People are naturally apprehensive regarding the possible misuse of power. Some Muslims, for example, complain that in certain places Christian groups have advanced and continue to advance their cause in South-East Asia by insensitive use of financial resources coming from the West. On the other hand, there are Christians who feel anxious about their position as a religious community in some places where political and/or financial power may belong predominantly to Muslims. Both Christians and Muslims ought readily to acknowledge that such accusations and apprehensions are not wholly unjustified on either side. In those places where assurances are needed and have not yet been given, both Christians and Muslims ought eagerly to affirm that neither community intends to misuse power to its own advantage.

The prerequisites of peace and humanity oblige both the Muslim and Christian communities to accept emotionally as well as intellectually the fact of their mutual existence in South-East Asia, with Muslims and

Christians recognizing each other as full and equal citizens of our national societies.

Christianity and Islam, along with Judaism, are in a special relationship with each other. We belong to the spiritual family of Abraham (*nabī Ibrāhīm*). We seek to be faithful and strive to be obedient in accordance with God's command and in response to God's grace or favour. We have many theological and ethical convergences and similarities. While in the not-so-distant past Christians and Muslims accentuated their differences to such a degree that some sectors in our respective communities regarded each other as unfriendly rivals, we now gratefully recognize that we are moving into a new era. In this new era our common ground is recognized as the context in which to understand our differences and we stretch out our hands in friendship and embrace each other as members of kindred communities of believers.

To be sure, Christians and Muslims possess distinctive elements in their respective faiths which they regard as precious treasures. Muslims have the Qur'an which in their belief and understanding is the revelation from God sent through his Messenger as a command, a light, a guidance, and a blessing for all people. Christians have the good news of the mighty acts of God in and through Jesus Christ for the redemption of mankind. A loving relationship with human beings leads Muslims and Christians to appreciate and respect these distinctive treasures of their respective faiths. Unfortunately, history provides some instances where Christians and Muslims sought coercively to impose their faiths on people who were resistant. Islam and Christianity, we believe, are in agreement that there can be no compulsion in religion. Wherever methods of compulsion, overt or covert, blatant or subtle, are still employed in order to draw people of one faith into another faith, these methods should be renounced as unworthy of Christianity and Islam.

Christians and Muslims both recognize it as a duty and a privilege to reduce areas of misunderstanding between their respective religious communities and between themselves and others, while all the time affirming the integrity and dignity of human beings. We affirm that all human relationships should point to God as the Beginning and the End of all things.

Two methods of fostering understanding especially commend themselves to us. The first of these entails witnessing in society to the highest and best in our respective religions by the example of our personal manner of life, behaviour, and worship. The second method involves us in engaging, in a spirit of goodwill, in discourse with all interested persons about the teachings of our respective religions.

Areas of common concern in social and political contexts

1. Varying situations of the relationships between our religious communities

We believe that God has a purpose for our communities, however different their respective situations. We believe that we should respond to his purpose by working together for a moral and just society; true prosperity cannot be achieved without the individual's personal commitment to morality and justice.

We live in a world where power is sometimes abused. At all levels of our societies we bear a responsibility to help establish the conditions for the right of power. Decision-making processes in the hands of responsible persons who are just and sensitive to the needs of all people will enhance the effective use of power. Muslims and Christians, like their other neighbours, often fail to live up to this responsibility, but we believe that we have a duty to strive individually and together to contribute to and to implement the aspirations of our respective religious communities.

Political harmony is precious to both communities. All human aspirations can best be realized under a condition of peace and order. However, such a climate can only be fully attained within a political and legal framework which ensures freedom and harmonious interaction for all religious communities. We commend the positive and creative role which governments may play in helping to reduce tensions and conflicts between religious communities.

Nevertheless, political stability can sometimes breed complacency. Muslims and Christians should remain alert to the way in which selfish tendencies can creep in. Freedom may be eroded and lost by subtle encroachments rather than by abrupt and dramatic aggression. This can happen when self-interest or group-interest predominates over the common welfare. Accordingly, Muslims and Christians should make a conscious effort to seek each other's assistance to defend their common interest and to work together in the service of their neighbours and of God.

We have tasks to perform even in situations where our religious communities may be politically weak or powerless, or where they may suffer formal or actual legal disabilities. One among these tasks is working together for reconciliation and reconstruction.

2. The response of religions to changing values in rapidly developing societies

Historically, Islam and Christianity have contributed much to the development of human societies, notably in the formulation of ethical values. However, there has been a tendency for social traditions and laws, embodying those values, to become too dogmatic or legalistic so as to be closed to worthwhile change as society has sought to respond to emergent needs. Moreover, to a certain extent our two religions have seemed to some sectors of society to be conservative and resistant to progress.

There are many who feel that religion is and ought to be an immovable anchor in rapidly changing social situations. But we feel that our fast changing societies are right to expect that Muslims and Christians should subject their own ethical values to careful scrutiny in the light of new situations which demand new duties and fresh responses. The spiritual and ethical foundations of our two faiths are the constant sources of light and guidance, but the situations upon which the light must shine and to which the guidance must be given are continually changing.

The response of our two religious communities to situations of rapid social change involves the mobilization of our resources for a variety of concerns, among which are: concern for the dignity of mankind and the basic rights of the individual; concern for social justice; concern for the character and shape of national consciousness; and concern for freedom in the choice and practice of religion.

Of special importance for our religious communities in some situations is the matter of proselytism. We are moved to call upon all religious bodies and individuals to refrain from proselytism, which we define as the compulsive, conscious, deliberate and tactical effort to draw people from one community of faith to another.

Our religions have the responsibility to alert society to religious, moral and spiritual values in the changing circumstances of daily life. Our responsibility is to enhance the total development of the human personality, spiritually and socially, and to stand squarely behind all that promotes justice and peace. Our religions are called upon to offer fresh motivations and fresh guidance for the growing expectations and changing aspirations of human beings in society.

Consultation and cooperation between our religious communities

Although no single political system can be applied to our diverse situations in South-East Asia, we do find a common range of mutual involvement and cooperation for our religious communities. In order to encourage responsible citizenship and participation in the lives of our respective nations, we recognize as areas of common concern and we commend as fruitful areas of consultation and cooperation at all levels of our societies the following:

a) common concern for the preservation of the rule of law, the mainte-
    nance of a free and responsible press, the safeguarding of academic
    freedom, and the affirmation and protection of human values in an
    expanding technological society;

b) striving to ensure for all sectors of our communities adequate partici-
    pation and fair representation in decision-making and the just exercise
    of power through responsible leadership;

c) striving to overcome the dangers that ideological forces can pose to
    our religious faiths and beliefs;

d) sharing a challenge and expectation to create a society which values
    and preserves the quality of life in terms of humanitarian and spiritual
    duties;

e) cooperation in encouraging responsible parenthood and measures for
    environmental control to preserve the ecological balance for future
    generations.

Cooperation in relief and rehabilitation

We deplore deliberate and unnecessary multiplication of competitive charitable organizations and social agencies. However, we warmly welcome the development of any initiative on the part of either community or both where such an initiative is needed and has due regard for human dignity and the religious sensitivities of the beneficiaries. For instance, where the relief is extended principally at the initiative of one religious community, distribution should be on the basis of need rather than affiliation. To accomplish this, consultation between the religious communities, whether donors or recipients, in the matters of planning, administration and implementation of relief programmes is imperative; otherwise misunderstanding and suspicion will ensue. These requirements of impartiality and partnership must equally apply in the no less urgent programmes of rehabilitation. All these efforts should avoid encouraging dependence, but should lead to self-reliance coupled with a spirit of constructive self-giving.

Even as we may undertake the present tasks of relief, rehabilitation and reconstruction in some of our societies we feel the urgency to plan ahead for programmes and measures which are directed towards avoidance in the future of possible tensions and other sources of conflict between our communities.

Some specific examples of Muslim-Christian collaboration in social work

1. *In Indonesia,* there exists the so-called Inter-religious Cooperation for Community Organization (ICCO). It is a local organization which is jointly run by Muslims and Christians. The motivation is to meet direct human needs. The organization operates in big cities like Jakarta, Surabaya and Semarang. In Jakarta, the area of activities is mainly concentrated in the new industrial slums of the northern part of the city, and the cooperation of the local city government is required. Funds, personnel and other facilities have been contributed by the religious groups and other private sources. Examples of social needs include family planning, housing problems, sanitation and teaching various skills to unemployed trishaw drivers who have been victims of the modernization of city traffic.

2. *In Malaysia,* Muslims and Christians with peoples of other faiths do joint study to see how they can advance together in the field of welfare; for example in 1973 a national seminar was organized by the government to help Muslim, Christian, and other voluntary organizations of the various faiths to see how they could best plan for their individual projects. In the same year, another national seminar was organized — the initiative was again taken by the government — to see how best Muslim, Christian, Buddhist, Hindu and other voluntary organizations, without prejudice to their internal autonomy, could maximize their efforts in nation-building in the face of changing values and structures in Malaysia.

In ventures taken by Christians, Muslims are members of the board of directors, advisers, committee members and staff members. There is inter-religious cooperation at all levels from the planning to the implementation of the project to serve the multi-racial and multi-religious needs of beneficiaries. In times of flood and other disasters, welfare work on a national basis is carried out under the sponsorship of the social welfare department in cooperation with religious and secular welfare agencies.

To promote peace in Malaysia there is the Malaysia Inter-Religious Organization, duly registered, the objects of which are:

a) to promote peace in Malaysia in particular and in the world in general;

b) to practise and spread the idea of the dignity of man and the spirit of brotherhood among all peoples by transcending the differences of race, nationality, sex, language or creed;

c) to practise and promote mutual understanding and cooperation among all religions.

3. *In the Philippines,* particularly in Mindanao and Sulu, there are Christian and Muslim organizations attending to the needs of the people (some of whom have been displaced by present tensions) regardless of religious affiliation. In Cotabato, joint ventures have been undertaken by the CORUM (Cotabato Rural Uplift Movement), the Notre Dame Social Action Centre, the Sultan Kudarat Islamic Teachers' Association and the Southern Diocesan Social Action Office. In Sulu, there is the Jolo Community Development Centre. These groups have often launched joint projects involving assistance in the form of food, shelter, and agricultural materials such as seeds, fertilizers and chemicals, work animals or tractor power. Joint efforts at providing for the housing need of Christians and Muslims on the low-income level are well exemplified by the Notre Dame village in Cotabato and the Kasanyangan Housing Cooperative in Jolo. The CORUM links up with the Consultative Council on Rurban (Rural-Urban) Development in its housing assistance for Muslim and Christian refugees.

4. *In Singapore,* bilateral Muslim-Christian relationships have been seen primarily within a multi-religious context. Since the relationships are set in a pragmatic society the concern has been for a fuller understanding of the life-style of an industrial society. The youth, for example, through the Singapore Inter-Religious Organization in conjunction with the Singapore Society of Spiritual Culture, have been helped by camps, seminars, and leadership training institutes to focus on actual social problems, to suggest areas of positive response, and to assume a responsible role in nation-building.

Religious education in pluralistic societies

Both Christians and Muslims recognize it as a duty to provide religious instruction for the young, emphasizing those elements which enrich life, show its significance and point to its final destiny in God. We realize that ways of religious instruction vary in the different countries of South-East Asia. In some there are government ministries responsible for this work. In others this responsibility is left to the parents or to the religious communities. While both communities hold that parents have a major responsibility for the religious instruction of their children, there is also a realistic appreciation that public and private education programmes can offer important opportunities for religious instruction. Indeed, in some places our respective communities have established schools of their own for just such purposes.

With respect to the latter, a question arises when a school is established by one religious community in a place inhabited predominantly by adherents of another religious community, and/or when there is a substantial enrolment of youngsters who are not from the faith of those who own and operate the school. The question is, what is the responsibility of the school for the religious instruction of children who come from families not of its faith? Whereas some will say that if a school is founded by people committed to a particular religious faith in order to be an instrument for the propagation of that faith, its responsibility is limited to teaching that religion only, we Muslims and Christians meeting at Hong Kong have another view. We believe that schools providing religious instruction for children from different religious communities should arrange to have such instruction given by qualified persons belonging to the respective communities. Christian children should receive religious instruction from a Christian, Muslim children from a Muslim, and so forth. We feel that it is a form of "compulsion in religion" for malleable, impressionable children in their formative years to be subject to religious training by instructors not of the faith of their parents.

This is not to say that there should be no place for the scientific study of religion. Both Islam and Christianity recognize that people have a duty to extend the frontiers of their knowledge and this includes knowledge of other religions besides their own. Moreover, because the study of religion is properly seen as an integral part of the total educational programme, courses in the philosophy, sociology, psychology and comparative study of religion may be offered at the higher levels of education in schools and colleges.

Building unity in diversity

The expression "unity in diversity" is well known in South-East Asian nations, all of which are faced initially at the national level with a task of forging common goals and a common identity from the rich variety of races, languages, cultures and religions within their national borders. The seal of the Republic of Indonesia bears the Sanskrit words *Bhinneka Tunggal Ika* which means "unity in diversity". The some 120 million Muslims and 47 million Christians who live with other neighbours in the lands of South-East Asia contribute significantly to the diversity of each nation and likewise have vital roles to play in the shape of national unity in their different places.

Because we belong to kindred communities of faith, there are doubtless many things which Christians and Muslims can do together to foster the unity of peoples in society. Among them we can identify the following:

1. Achieve and maintain peace between themselves, since not only national unity but regional stability are both advanced when the different religious communities live together in peace and harmony.
2. Witness together for the religious and moral perspective that respects the dignity and worth of all human beings in the face of dehumanizing forces.
3. Unite together to strengthen the moral conscience of national endeavour — affirming those aspects of nation-building which operate for the common good and, in obedience to God's will, calling attention to those aspects which are harmful or oppressive.
4. Promote together a human appreciation of the cultural achievements of all the diverse communities which make up the society — valuing those worthy achievements as the common property of the whole nation and of humanity.
5. Represent together the transcendent dimension of human beings in mundane society of men and women, old and young, who, in the final analysis, belong not only to this world of time and matter, but also to the Eternal.

Participants

Muslims invited for dialogue

Indonesia

Haji Syamsuddin Abdullah
Fak. Usuluddin,
IAIN "Sunan Kalijaga"
Jalan Adisucipto
Yogyakarta, Indonesia

Haji Rosihan Anwar
Jalan Surabaya 13
Jakarta Pusat, Indonesia

Dr Zakiah Darajat
Direktur Direktorat Pendidikan Agama
Kentor: Department Agama
Jalan M.H. Thamrin
Jakarta, Indonesia

Dr Harun Nasution
Hidayatullah, IAIN — Syarif
Jalan Ciputat, Kebayoran Lama
Jakarta, Indonesia

Malaysia

Tuan Haji Razali bin Haji Nawawi
Faculty of Islamic Studies
Universiti Kebangsaan Malaysia
Jalan Universiti
Petaling Jaya, Malaysia

Haji Faisal bin Haji Othman
Faculty of Islamic Studies
Universiti Kebangsaan Malaysia
Jalan Universiti
Petaling Jaya, Malaysia

Syed Ibrahim bin Syed Abdul Rahman
No. 167, Jalan Limau Purut
Bandar Raya
Kuala Lumpur, Malaysia

Dr Mohd. Yusof
Faculty of Islamic Studies
Universiti Kebangsaan
Petaling Jaya, Malaysia

Philippines

Miss Pian T. Albar
Jolo Community Development Project
Notre Dame of Jolo College
Jolu, Sulu, Philippines

Prof. Alunan C. Glang
5 Masunurin Street
Sikatuna Village
Quezon City, Philippines

Dr Cesar Adib Majul
Dean, Institute of Islamic Studies
Philippine Centre for Advanced
Studies, University of the Philippines
Diliman, Quezon City
Philippines

Attorney Michael O. Mastura
5-B Masunurin Street
Sikatuna Village
Quezon City, Philippines

Senator Mamintal A. Tamano
(co-chairman)
Suite 510 Ermita Centre
Roxas Boulevard
Manila, Philippines

CHRISTIANS INVITED FOR DIALOGUE

Hong Kong

Father Louis Lee
The Bishop's House
16 Caine Road, Hong Kong

Dr Peter Lee
Christian Study Centre
Tao Fong Shan, P.O. Box 33
Shatin, NT, Hong Kong

Mr Bartholomew Tsui
Chung Chi College
Chinese University of Hong Kong
Shatin, NT, Hong Kong

Indonesia

Dr Peter Latuihamallo (co-chairman)
Jalan Proklamasi 27
Jakarta-Pusat, Indonesia

Prof. Dr Ihromi
Jalan Proklamasi 27
Jakarta-Pusat, Indonesia

Mr Pontas Nasution
Institute Oikoumene Indonesia
JL. Salemba Raya 10
Jakarta, Indonesia

Rev. M.A. Simandjuntak
Christian Conference of Asia
480 Lorong 2, Toa Payoh
Singapore 19

Malaysia

Mr C.V. Das
M/S Shook Lin & Bok
Advocates and Solicitors
Lee Wah Bank Building
Medan Pasar
Kuala Lumpur, Malaysia

Rev. K. Jambunathan
St Barnabas Church
4 Jalan Sultan, Kelang
Selangor, Malaysia

Mr V.D.P. Pillai
Honorary Secretary, Diocesan Council
Evangelical Lutheran Church
of Malaysia and Singapore
21 Jalan Abdul Samad, Brickfields
Kuala Lumpur 0907, Malaysia

Rt Rev. Basil Temengong
Bishop's House, Kuching
Sarawak, Malaysia

Sister Theresa Thong
Good Shepherd Convent
5 ½ miles Ulu Klang Road
Kuala Lumpur, Malaysia

Pakistan

Dr Byron L. Haines
Christian Study Centre
128 Saifullah Lodhi Road
Rawalpindi, Pakistan

Philippines

Rev. Fr. Jose D. Ante
OMI, President
Notre Dame of Jolo College
Jolo, Sulu, Philippines

Fr Ruben Gomez
Oblate Novitiate
Tamontaka, Cotabato City
Philippines

Dr Peter G. Gowing
Director, Dansalan Research Centre
P.O. Box 5430
Iligan City 8801, Philippines

Mrs Portia R. Mapanao
Executive Director, Cotabato
Rural Uplift Movement, Midsayap
North Cotabato, Philippines

Rt Rev. Constancio B. Manguramas
P.O. Box 113
Cotabato City, Philippines 9301

Rev. Dr Robert McAmis
P.O. Box 507
Manila, Philippines

Singapore

Dr Tony Chi
Trinity College, 7 Mount Sophia
Singapore 9

Staff members

Mrs Monique McClellan
Chung Chi College
Shatin, NT, Hong Kong

Dr Stanley J. Samartha
Director, Dialogue with People
of Living Faiths and Ideologies
World Council of Churches
150 route de Ferney
1211 Geneva 20, Switzerland

Dr John B. Taylor
Assistant Director, Dialogue with
People of Living Faiths and Ideologies
World Council of Churches

Planning Together
1975-1983

II. 1

Christian Mission and Islamic Da'wah

Islam and Christianity are missionary faiths; among the adherents of both there is a desire to share the riches of the faith and the heritage with others. But it is notorious that, in the attempt to fulfill this missionary vocation, missionary activities of Christians among Muslims, and of Muslims among Christians, have sometimes led to grievances on both sides; both groups have long memories of past pressures to conform or more recent experiences of aggressive and insensitive proselytism.

With the unhappy events in the Lebanon and Mindanao and the growing tensions in other parts of the world demonstrating how urgent it is today to create conditions of understanding and mutual respect, we felt that the least we could do was to try to contribute to the elimination of the religious passions which further enflame conflicts basically due, much of the time, to economic, ideological or political differences.

On 26 June, with the cooperation of the two co-convenors, Dr David Kerr, director of the Centre for the Study of Islam and Christian-Muslim Relations and lecturer in Islam at the Selly Oak Colleges, Birmingham, and a sympathetic student of Islam, and Prof. Khurshid Ahmad, Leicester, director general of the Islamic Foundation, formerly professor of economics at the University of Karachi and a man well-acquainted with the Christian world, we called together a group of Christians and Muslims concerned with the fulfilment of their respective missionary obligations for a five-day consultation on Christian Mission and Islamic *da'wah*.

● This text first appeared in the *International Review of Mission* (IRM), Vol. LXV, No. 260, October 1976.

We as Christians cannot surrender our missionary vocation nor our commitment to the proclamation of the gospel. But the same missionary compulsion to engagement in *da'wah* belongs to our Muslim neighbours out of their own religious heritage and from their religious convictions. The group tried to explain to each other their basic motivations, to understand and if possible to correct the caricatures they had of one another, and to see how damaging realities could be changed and a pattern of behaviour in mission and *da'wah* defined and commended. The encounter was an impassioned one, in which it was not easy to agree. At the same time, however, time and time again, we came back to the conference table with the conviction that ways could and should be found to create more fruitful situations for reciprocal witness.

Working on a draft prepared originally by the Muslim participants, the group was able to hammer out a general expression of agreement. This document might have reflected other approaches to the matter — more radical, or more daring, or more conservative. But its value lies in the fact that it is not just an expression of our Christian understanding of how mission could or should be carried out among adherents of the Muslim religion, or vice versa, but that together, Christians and Muslims affirmed basic principles concerning the freedom to exercise one's religion, to propagate one's faith, "the right to convince and be convinced" and deplored those things which stand in the way of the exercise of such freedom.

For me, who had had little previous contact with Muslims and the world of Islam, the discussions, the papers and not least the human contacts were an illuminating experience. We believe that you will find much to think about in this issue of the IRM. Now the editorial word belongs to our two friends, and the co-editors of this issue, Khurshid Ahmad and David Kerr.

EMILIO CASTRO

* * *

In the name of Allah, the Merciful, the Mercy-Giving.

> SAY: "People of the Book, (let us) rally to common terms, to be binding on both, us and you, that we shall worship only God (alone) and associate nothing else with Him, nor shall any of us take others as lords instead of God."
> The Qur'an 3:64

Perhaps this is the first time that a Muslim has acted as a co-editor for a special issue of the IRM. On the face of it, this may appear to be a small step, yet it may go a long way in improving the state of religious co-existence: moving from co-existence towards pro-existence and greater cooperation between the family of Abraham (peace be upon him). The initiative for the present effort came from the Commission on World Mission and Evangelism of the World Council of Churches and the IRM, to which the Muslims have responded in good faith.

After working on this project for almost one year, I, for one, have no regrets for having entered these uncharted waters. We met and worked together as people committed to serve God alone, and as persons resolved to live in accordance with the religious values and traditions we firmly believe in. We hold no brief for syncretism, nor were we interested in producing compromises on matters religious and moral. Similarly, we did not enter the consultation with a view to scoring points on each other. We met with the objective of understanding each other's position more sympathetically, of identifying the areas of agreement and disagreement and of trying to build mutual trust so as to coordinate our response to threats and challenges that beset humanity today. Instead of merely talking about each other, we have tried to talk to each other, however haltingly. That is why we, instead of producing an impersonal collection of scholarly papers, have tried to collect around one table a few distinguished religious leaders of the two faiths and invite them to face each other as much as face the real issues that confront them. The fruits of this lively encounter are presented in this special issue on Christian Mission and Islamic *da'wah*.

It is our considered opinion that the right approach in Christian-Muslim dialogue is to face the problems and issues that unite or divide us. These issues are legion: religious, theological, historical, socio-cultural, political. As mission/*da'wah* represents the outreach of one's religious tradition to the other and as the role of Christian missions in the Muslim world is regarded by the Muslims to be at the root of estrangement between the Christian and the Muslim worlds, the conference on mission and *da'wah* provided a natural point of departure for a meaningful dialogue.

Although there have been moments of stress and strain, expressions of human weakness and pugnacity, even wars and political encounters, Christians and Muslims have lived side by side in the Muslim world, on the whole, in peace and harmony with each other, ever since the final revelation of Islam in the seventh century.

But with the arrival of the Christian missionaries in the company of European colonizers, a new chapter began in Muslim-Christian relationships. That some of them might have been motivated by the best of spiritual intentions is not among the points of dispute. But the overall Muslim experience of the Christian mission was such that it failed to commend itself as something noble and holy. Any dispassionate evaluation of the experience would suggest that what has been achieved is a loss for Islam and religion as such, and not a gain for Christianity — the real beneficiaries being the forces of secularism, materialism and of moral insensitivity. The Muslim critique can be summed up in four points:

a) Gross and flagrant misrepresentation of the teachings of Islam and of the life and message of the Prophet Muhammad (peace be upon him). Instead of examining Islam as it is, a totally unreal picture of Islam was concocted and used to denigrate Islam and Muslims. Although the high watermark of this type of approach to the study of Islam has passed, the effort still persists, even though in low profile and under many a disguise.

b) The methodology of Christian mission concentrated upon influencing the object in a state of weakness and helplessness. Instead of direct invitation, approaches were made to those who were disadvantaged, exploiting their weaknesses for the sake of proselytism. The poor, the sick and the immature were made special targets of economic assistance, medical aid and education. Many a Christian mission acted as an organic part of colonialism and cultural imperialism. All this was a very unfair way to bring people to any religion.

c) Whatever the ultimate aim, subversion of the faith and culture of Islam seems to have been the prime target of the Christian missionary enterprise. Nationalism, secularism, modernism, socialism, even communism were fostered, supported and encouraged. While the revival of Islam and the strengthening of Islamic moral life among the Muslims were, and even now are, looked upon as anathema.

d) Muslims were treated as political rivals and as such subjected to overt and covert discrimination and repression. Their just causes fail to evoke any significant moral response from the Christian world. Western Christendom's attitude towards the Palestine problem in general and towards Jerusalem in particular, for example, agonizes Muslims. Majority rule is denied to Muslims in a number of African countries. The sufferings of the Muslims in such places as Eritrea, Mindanao, Kashmir, Patani, to mention only a few, fail sufficiently to arouse the moral conscience of the Christian world. Muslims are puzzled when they compare the relative lack of Christian concern over the increasing de-

Christianization of the Christian world with their obsession with what amounts to de-Islamization of the Muslim world.

This being the nature of the Muslim concern it was but natural that any meaningful dialogue must begin with a review of the Christian and Muslim positions in respect of the whole experience of mission and *da'wah*. The conference concentrated upon two major aspects of the problem: the fundamental position of Islam and Christianity in respect of *da'wah* and mission and the Christian and Muslim experience of each other's missionary/*da'wah* activity. Both religions are light-sharing. But there are differences in the way they offer their message to others, at a deeper level, in the way they concern themselves with the world.

The two sections on the nature and concept of the Christian mission and Islamic *da'wah* and the discussions that follow bring this into sharp focus. The missionary experience of the two communities too has its disparities. A careful perusal of the material presented here will show that three issues emerge distinctly from the debate:

First, there has been widespread abuse of Christian diakonia and something effective needs to be done to bring an end to that. Secondly, the whole question of secularism and Westernization has to be studied in the context of religio-historical traditions of Islam and Christianity. Greater sensitivity needs to be shown to differences in the religious ideals and the historical situations of the Christian West and the Muslim world. Thirdly, although human freedom is even more essential for the flowering of man's spiritual and religious life than for his political existence, freedom becomes meaningful only within a framework of commitments and responsibilities. As such, equal concern should be shown towards the freedom and integrity of the individual and the solidarity of the community.

With these key issues in perspective, the importance of the conference statement becomes clear. Although representing the consensus of a few persons, its significance lies in the fact that it can show the way to a more universal consensus. Its uniqueness lies in the spirit of frankness and fairness in which it is offered. It represents an attitude of loyalty to God and not necessarily to one's "tribe"; acceptance of facts, whether pleasant or unpleasant; and respect for the viewpoint and the feelings of others. With such an approach, man can move towards a new world of mutuality and pro-existence. If this is what we are aiming at, then the Chambésy statement could be a milestone.

What about the future? The Chambésy spirit and the concrete suggestions it frames represent a first step on a long and arduous road men of goodwill from Christianity and Islam will have to tread if they want to change Christian-Muslim relations for the better. The mini-consensus evolved at Chambésy deserves to be *widened* as well as *deepened*. It contains the seeds from which the tree of some universal consensus can grow. To deepen the consensus, efforts should be made to organize a series of conferences, seminars, conventions and colloquia at different levels with a view to developing better understanding of each other's religious and historical tradition; to frame ethical rules governing dialogue, cooperation and even healthy competition; to jointly produce works of serious scholarship and frank encounters and to participate jointly in centres and institutions devoted to serving these purposes. Along with widening and deepening the consensus, effective steps should be taken to implement the proposals contained in the statement. This is an area where organizations like the World Council of Churches, the Vatican, the Islamic Secretariat, the Muslim World League, The Call of Islam Society, the Islamic Council of Europe and the like can make some significant contribution not only in healing the wounds and clearing the debris but also in building new bridges to bring the family of Abraham closer in love and mutual trust. If the Chambésy conference and the present efforts of the IRM, the Islamic Foundation and the Centre for the Study of Islam and Christian-Muslim Relations in Europe could make some opening in that direction, this small step could be the precursor of a great change.

KHURSHID AHMAD
The Islamic Foundation, Leicester, England

* * *

This conference on Christian Mission and Islamic *da'wah* may well mark the first occasion in the history of Christian-Muslim relations of members of the two faiths meeting, albeit informally, to discuss an area of commitment which is fundamental to their respective faiths; for *da'wah* is to Islam as mission is to Christianity, and of the latter Dr Samartha has written in an earlier issue of this journal, "to reject mission is to take out the oil of the lamp". The issue of mission and *da'wah* has of course arisen in earlier meetings between Muslims and Christians, and some of the implications for practical relationships have been recognized and commended for further discussion. But never before, to my knowledge, have Christians and Muslims met together at an international level to address themselves explicitly to this vital issue which is elemental to the integrity of both.

This fact in itself makes the conference one of significance, whatever conclusions individuals may draw from reading the record of proceedings in the pages following. The CWME and IRM are to be congratulated for the boldness of their initiative in calling the conference into being, and I know I speak for all the participants in expressing thanks for the depth of concern shown, and the warmth of hospitality extended by those responsible.

The absolute commitment of the Christian mission and of the Muslim to *da'wah* has undoubtedly been one of the principal contributory factors to the tension, and at times conflict, which has so extensively characterized the relationship between Christianity and Islam. Each feels itself to have been abused by the other, though not necessarily in the same way, and the pains of grievance continue to this day, with Muslims — I believe with justification — incensed to the point of outrage by certain aspects of Christian action in the name of mission. To this the following pages bear ample witness. Some Christian participants in the discussions, amongst whom I include myself, may have felt that Muslim sensitivity to the breadth of new missionary thought and action within Christianity was dulled by their very justified anger with other practices which, though older, are by no means dead. Nonetheless I urge all Christian readers to take to heart, in humility and with utter seriousness, the grievances expressed by the Muslim participants. The experience of this conference has left me convinced that however well-intentioned and well-informed Christians may be about Islam, rarely are they sufficiently sensitive to the depth and implications of the Muslim sense of injury at the hand of the Christian missionary.

The conference discussion was intense throughout, and at times emotions erupted in a manner painful to Muslims and Christians alike. Perhaps this is as it should have been in a first conference on mission and *da'wah*, which could in no way abstract itself from the burden of mistrust which besets the missionary relationship between Muslim and Christian. Certainly the Christian participants wish to record their gratitude to the Muslims for accepting to enter into this encounter, given the fact that each Muslim participant has had, in various ways, personal experience of Western Christian missionaries which has left him suspicious of Christian motives in mission and reluctant to engage in discussion with missionaries. Gratitude must also be expressed for the honesty with which the Muslims spoke — an honesty manifestly inspired by the desire for improved relations in the future.

In planning the conference it seemed desirable, in the interests of intimacy of discussion, to restrict the number of participants to six Muslims and six Christians, in addition to the two co-editors and certain WCC staff members, and to invite participants experienced in missionary encounter with people of the other faith in parts of the world where Islam and Christianity are in daily contact.

Unfortunately not all who had been invited were, in the event, able to attend. The absence of Prof. Ishtiaq Qureshi, formerly vice-chancellor of the University of Karachi, Pakistan, was deeply regretted. An Islamic scholar and spokesman of such repute, and one so well read in Christianity, with long personal experience of Christian mission work, would certainly have brought valuable perspectives to the discussion, but of this benefit the conference was deprived through insoluble technical difficulties.

The inability, at the eleventh hour, of Dr Subhi Saleh and Metropolitan Georges Khodre to travel from Beirut was a further sorely-felt loss to the conference. The agony of the present protracted conflict between Christians and Muslims in Lebanon was amongst the considerations which made the calling of a conference such as this urgent. And it was precisely because the shadow of Lebanese events haunted with such chill the consciences of all, that the conference ached from the absence of a Lebanese voice, and particularly the voices of the two Lebanese we had wanted to hear.

Discussion throughout the first half of the conference centred around formal papers commissioned from several Christian and Muslim participants, and circulated to all participants in advance. These papers, in which the writers presented their personal understandings of Christian mission and Islamic *da'wah*, and also certain case studies of Muslim experience of mission and Christian experience of *da'wah* (with attention to both the historical and the contemporary), are here published in the order in which they were given. To each paper a Muslim and a Christian participant were invited to respond in prelude to a "round-the-table" discussion in which the issues were developed in such ways as participants felt most fruitful, under the guidance of the chair which was held by different participants in turn. The latter part of the conference was given to a consideration of ways whereby Christians and Muslims could seek to improve their practical relationship while at the same time retaining their imperative commitments to mission and *da'wah*. This led, if somewhat hesitantly, to the preparation of a final document which is generally expressive of the concerns and hopes of the participants, though some would not wish it to be read as a statement of their personal views on all subjects mentioned, of which certain receive little if any discussion round the table. All the discussion was recorded and is available on tapes, from which the co-editors subsequently extracted and edited a sequence of excerpts which, in their opinion, contain the most interesting material for a general readership.

The co-editors humbly offer their work in the succeeding pages, with all its imperfections, in the belief that the participants in the discussions in Chambésy have contributed in a small but significant way to the cause of greater understanding between two great missionary faiths. One could have wished for better results, the fruit of a more searching, questing, mutually-relating enterprise of partly-common, always loyal minds. But what we have raises many issues for our future consideration, and may cause us to question inherited assumptions about mission and *da'wah*.

This conference has taught me much which I believe to be important in dialogue between men of living faiths; notably, that if our commitment to "togetherness" is persistent, this itself can contain the sharp and at times angry controversy of inter-religious debate, which may then be turned to productive result. This conference must lay once and for all the suspicion of the sceptic that dialogue is a passing of courtesies; it never has been, and after this conference it never will be. Furthermore, I believe the conference brings sharply before the attention of Christians the need to reflect with greater clarity upon the proper relationship between mission and dialogue, in recognition that we are living in a situation not simply of plurality of religions, but of plurality of missions. How we cope with this situation, at once critically and openly, is an issue which calls urgently for the consideration of missiologist and missionary alike.

In conclusion I would thank, with deep gratitude of a friendship matured through experiences such as here recorded, my co-editor, Brother Khurshid, whose resources of energy are matched only by his patient disposition towards his younger colleague.

DAVID KERR

Centre for the Study of Islam and Christian-Muslim Relations
Selly Oak Colleges, Birmingham, England

* * *

Statement of the conference

The last day of the consultation was spent in the preparation of a final document for publication in the IRM along with the formal papers and excerpts of the discussions. In order to speed this undertaking two working papers were drafted, one by the Christians and the other by the Muslims, in which each group set out its consensus opinion. When the plenary session reconvened it was decided to adopt the more detailed Muslim papers as a basis for the combined document, and various revisions in the form of amendments, deletions and additions were then discussed and agreed. The participants requested the editors to undertake the techical editing of the final version which appears below.

The final document reflects some of the concerns and hopes felt by the participants. The participants were invited to Geneva in order to consult together as people experienced in Christian mission and Islamic da'wah, *and knowledgeable of each other's traditions, and it is in this spirit that the document seeks to draw together some of the main themes of the consultation, and to raise issues for the further consideration of interested parties.* (Editors)

1. In recognition that mission and *da'wah* are essential religious duties in both Christianity and Islam, a conference on Christian mission and Islamic *da'wah* was organized by the Commission on World Mission and Evangelism of the World Council of Churches, Geneva, in consultation with the Islamic Foundation, Leicester, and the Centre for the Study of Islam and Christian-Muslim Relations, Selly Oak Colleges, Birmingham, on 11 Jumada 28-Rajab 4, 1396/26-30 June 1976. Beside examining the nature of mission and of *da'wah*, and the experience of each community of the missionary/*da'wah* activity of the other, the purpose of the conference was to promote reciprocal understanding between Muslims and Christians and to explore the means for a *modus vivendi* assuring the spiritual wellbeing of all.

2. The conference is in essential agreement that their respective communities, wherever they constitute a minority of the population, should enjoy a *de jure* existence; that each religious community should be entitled to live its religious life in accordance with its religion in perfect freedom. The conference upholds the principle of religious freedom recognizing that the Muslims as well as the Christians much enjoy the full liberty to convince and be convinced, and to practise their faith and order their religious life in accordance with their own religious laws and principles; that the individual is perfectly entitled to maintain his/her

religious integrity in obedience to his/her religious principles and in faithfulness to his/her religious identity.

3. The conference agrees that the family is a supremely precious and necessary institution. It expresses serious concern over the threats of disintegration and secularization facing the family institution, and it recommends that religious family law, whether Muslim or Christian, be not interfered with or changed in any way, directly or indirectly, by outsiders to their traditions. It also agrees that the family and community should have the right to ensure the religious education of their children by organizing their own schools, or by having teachers of their own denominations to teach religion to their children in the school, or by other suitable means. In any case they should be allowed to organize their cultural and spiritual life without outside interference, though with sensitivity to the situation of multi-religious societies.

4. The conference was grieved to hear that some Christians in some Muslim countries have felt themselves limited in the exercise of their religious freedom and have been denied their right to church buildings. The Muslim participants regard such violation as contrary to Islamic law as well as to the principle of religious freedom enunciated above.

5. The conference recognizes fully the right of Christians as well as of Muslims to order their corporate life in accordance with the injunctions of their own religious principles and laws, and to have and maintain all requisite institutions in accordance with their religious principles and laws as equal citizens.

6. The Christian participants extend to their Muslim brethren their full sympathy for the moral wrongs which the Muslim world has suffered at the hands of colonialists, neo-colonialists and their accomplices. The conference is aware that Muslim-Christian relations have been affected by mistrust, suspicion and fear. Instead of cooperating for the common good, Muslims and Christians have been estranged and alienated from one another. After more than a century of colonialism during which many missionaries served the interests of the colonial powers, whether deliberately or unconsciously, the Muslims have felt reluctant to cooperate with the Christians whom they have fought as agents of their oppressors. Although the time has certainly come to turn a new page in this relationship, the Muslims are still reluctant to take the step because their suspicion of Christian intentions continues. The reason is the undeniable fact that many of the Christian missionary services today continue to be undertaken for ulterior motives. Taking advantage of Muslim ignorance, of Muslim need for education, health, cultural and social services, of

Muslim political stresses and crises, of their economic dependence, political division and general weakness and vulnerability, these missionary services have served purposes other than holy — proselytism, that is, adding members to the Christian community for reasons other than spiritual. Recently revealed linkages of some of these services with the intelligence offices of some big powers confirm and intensify an already aggravated situation. The conference strongly condemns all such abuse of diakonia (service). Its Christian members dissociate themselves in the name of Christianity from any service which has degraded itself by having any purpose whatever beside *agapé* (love for God and neighbour). They declare that any diakonia undertaken for any ulterior motive is a propaganda instrument and not an expression of *agapé*. They agree to exercise their full power and use whatever means at their disposal to bring Christian churches and religious organizations to a proper awareness of this situation.

7. The conference, being painfully aware that Muslim attitudes to Christian mission have been so adversely affected by the abuse of diakonia, strongly urges Christian churches and religious organizations to suspend their misused diakonia activities in the world of Islam. Such a radical measure is necessary to cleanse the atmosphere of Muslim-Christian relations and orientate them towards mutual recognition and cooperation worthy of the two great religions. The conference urges strongly that all material assistance donated by outside churches and religious organizations henceforth be distributed wherever possible through or in cooperation with the governments and local communities of people for whom they are intended, respecting the dignity and integrity of the people concerned.

8. The conference urges that soon after the measures mentioned in the two preceding paragraphs begin to be implemented, Muslims and Christians should be invited to an assembly representative of the two faiths to consider the methods of mission and *da'wah*, and the rules pertinent to each religion, and to seek modalities for enabling each religion to exercise its missionary call/*da'wah* in accordance with its own faith. The conference recognizes that mission and *da'wah* are essential religious duties of both Christianity and Islam, and that the suspension of misused diakonia services is to the end of re-establishing mission in the future on a religiously sound basis acceptable to both. Such an assembly may also establish permanent organs with Christian and Muslim participation for the purpose of preventing or dealing with aberrations or violations of Muslim/Christian understanding by either party.

9. The conference is aware that good neighbourly and cooperative relations between Christians and Muslims cannot exist or endure unless there is a deep-anchored reciprocal understanding of theologies, histories, moral and legal doctrines, social and political theories and problems of acculturation and modernization faced by the two faiths. To this end the conference urges that the World Council of Churches, the Vatican and the international Islamic organizations sponsor conferences at which these themes will be examined and discussed at regular intervals.

10. The conference, and especially the Muslim participants, express their deep and heartfelt appreciation to the WCC and the editors of the IRM for calling and sponsoring this conference. All participants express their joy that God has granted them the grace to bear in patience and empathize with one another. They are thankful to God that this conference may have made some contribution towards purifying the atmosphere of Muslim-Christian relations, and they pray that relations between their people may soon blossom into spiritual fellowship, to the glory of God alone.

Participants

Mr Khurshid Ahmad is director general of the Islamic Foundation, Leicester.

Bishop Kenneth Cragg lectures in the University of Sussex, England, and is Episcopal Assistant Bishop in Jerusalem and the Middle East.

Dr Isma'il R. al-Faruqi is professor of Islamic studies, Temple University, Philadelphia.

Father Michael Fitzgerald is director of the Pontificio Istituto di Studi Arabi in Rome.

Prof. Joseph Hajjar, a Greek-Catholic expert in canon law and church history, with specialization in the history of Muslim-Christian relations in the Near East, teaches in Damascus, Syria.

Prof. Ihromi is rector of Sekolah Tinggi Theologia, Jakarta, Indonesia.

Mr A. Irfan is editor of *Impact International*, London.

Dr David Kerr is lecturer in Islamics, Selly Oak Colleges, Birmingham, and director of the Centre for the Study of Islam and Christian-Muslim Relations.

Mr Ali Muhsin Barwani, former deputy prime minister and minister for external affairs in the government of Zanzibar, leader of the Zanzibar Nationalist Party and editor of the *Mwongozim*, a weekly paper, now lives in Cairo.

Dr Ishtiaq Quraishi, of the University of Karachi, was at the last minute unable to attend the consultation.

Dr Muhammed Rasjidi, former minister of religious affairs of the government of Indonesia, is presently professor of Islamic studies, University of Indonesia, Jakarta.

Bishop Arne Rudvin, bishop of the United Church of Pakistan, lives in Karachi.

Dr Subhi Saleh, Vice-Mufti of Lebanon, was at the last minute unable to attend the consultation.

Dr Lamin Sanneh is lecturer in the Department of Religious Studies, University of Legon, Ghana, and research adviser to the Islam in Africa Project.

Observers

The Rev. Emilio Castro is director of the Commission on World Mission and Evangelism of the WCC and editor of the *International Review of Mission*.

Dr John Taylor is associate for Christian-Muslim relations in the programme for Dialogue with People of Living Faiths and Ideologies, WCC.

II. 2
Next Steps
in Christian-Muslim Dialogue

In order to plan together the next steps in Christian-Muslim dialogue, 12 Christians and 12 Muslims conferred with WCC staff at Cartigny, Geneva, 19-22 October 1976. Some of the participants were invited as concerned individuals with previous involvements in Muslim-Christian dialogue. Others were representatives or observers from international, regional or local Muslim or Christian bodies.

The meeting started by hearing the personal experiences and expectations of the participants. Their experiences ranged from the easy relations between Christians and Muslims in the same family in West Africa to the currently shattered achievements of Christian-Muslim coexistence in Lebanon. Their expectations ranged from the encouragement of mutually respectful and sometimes self-critical inter-religious understanding to urgent pleas for reconciliation where violence or mistrust has divided Muslims and Christians from each other.

A. Preparation for dialogue within both communities
The participants acknowledged the need for continuing preparations for dialogue to be encouraged at all possible levels within their own communities. An important enabling and supportive role for such preparations might be played by Christian and Muslim international, regional and local bodies as well as by individuals.

It was felt that despite an increasing range of initiatives from both Muslim and Christian sides at international, regional and local levels, there was still a major problem in that many Muslims and Christians still distrusted the idea of dialogue. However, it was recognized that participation in dialogue itself offers one way of removing suspicions and building up a climate of understanding, friendliness and mutual trust. It was felt that any plans for next steps in dialogue should be commended to the Muslim and Christian communities with a statement of the aims of such dialogues.

Such a statement of aims could help to dispel suspicions and frustrations as well as illustrating the rich variety of experiences and aspirations held by Christian and Muslim partners in dialogue. At present it seems premature to define or even to attempt exhaustive descriptions of the wide variety of experiences and aspirations held by Christians and Muslim partners in dialogue. Acknowledging the helpful elements in many of the definitions and descriptions of the objectives of Muslims on previous occasions, such as Cartigny 1969, Broumana 1972 and Tripoli 1976, the present group recognized that the following principles are important:

Each partner should aim to achieve:
— understanding of common and distinctive elements in each other's faith, history and civilization;
— respect for each other's religious and cultural integrity;
— common commitment to strive for social justice and for responsible development of the earth's resources;
— a mutually challenging enrichment of spirituality which may also be a challenge to secular neighbours.

Each partner should aim to avoid:
— unfair comparison or caricature;
— any attempt to impose a syncretistic solution;
— complacency about a static coexistence;
— defensive and hostile attitudes to secular neighbours.

B. Living in dialogue

1. Dialogue is often conceived as a matter of conversation among experts or of cooperation between organizations. Yet dialogue often begins as part of the daily experience of men and women, old and young in both our communities. Three areas of encounter were discussed in particular detail: education, family life, and worship and prayer.

2. The meeting proposed a series of considerations, and recommendations:

a) Education
   The three areas of schools, teachers and textbooks call for various forms of action, most of which can be implemented at the local level,

although some may call for the stimulus or cross-fertilization afforded by regional or international meetings or projects.

i) Schools should be on a locality rather than strictly denominational basis, where both communities of faith are living side by side. Parents and teachers of both groups should cooperate in the management of the schools and thus help to build up one local community.

ii) Teachers should be fully informed about both faiths. Each community of faith should be encouraged to have an open mind towards its neighbours of the other faith and should receive appropriate instruction about it. Many religious people believe that religious instruction should be given to the children of each religious group by a practising member of that religion, with a sympathetic understanding towards the other faith.

iii) Textbooks for religious instruction should be prepared through consultation and cooperation between the two groups, and should contain no material unacceptable to either.

b) Family life

Dialogue is possible only where there is an openness and accommodation towards minority cultures. *There should be encouragement of community sources* helping to bring families into closer contact, and catering for special needs, especially for youth, *maybe in the organizing of study groups, social projects, youth camps, etc.* This should help to build mutual respect between the two communities of faith.

Deliberate efforts should be made to include more women participants in future dialogue meetings. *Conversations among women of both faiths should be encouraged at the regional level, sponsored by both Christian and Muslim organizations.*

c) Worship and prayer

We all note the distinction between formal worship (for Muslims, *Salat*) and prayer (for Muslims, *Dua*). *We encourage appropriate sharing in the celebration of each other's festivals.* Some of us have been willing to allow silent presence of each other's worship times. Some of us have shared in prayer of supplication and meditation and have prayed for each other since we all pray to the One God and believe that He is in our dialogue.

Despite hesitations and difficulties, we should be open to learn from each other as we submit our own finite faith to God's guidance.

C. Dialogue on socio-political issues

1. Certain issues call for clarification within our dialogue.

a) Faith and politics in Islamic and Christian thought

Muslims and Christians live in differing contexts across the world. Sometimes they are a majority and sometimes a minority, perhaps in an Islamic state, perhaps in a secular state, perhaps in a democratic state, perhaps in a totalitarian state. How far are they victims of structural violence whether from the weight of history, the international environment or the mass media? How do they envisage ways to regulate and construct their society in accordance with the teaching of their faith?

What is the role of Islam and, in particular, what is the role of Ijtihad (disciplined interpretation) in the formulation and the application of the principle of equal rights and opportunities to all citizens in the state? Especially where Christians live with Muslim majorities they should ask themselves how they envisage their role as citizens. How far are both Muslims' and Christians' faiths challenged by and how far may they both act as a challenge to modern society?

b) Social justice and development

How can Christians and Muslims act together in order to realize throughout their societies the Christian and Islamic ideals of social justice and integral human development? How can they engage in non-violent struggle against unjust forces and how can they narrow the widening gulf between rich and poor groups and nations? Can Muslim and Christian scholars cooperate in defining the rights of individuals and groups to enjoy social and political justice?

2. These two areas call for *initiatives from international Christian and Islamic organizations and from regional and local Christian and Muslim bodies*. In particular the group recommends that:

a) Faith and politics in Islam

Seminars should be arranged in order to stimulate analysis and improve understanding, not least among Christians, about *Islamic principles and practice of organization of the state*.

b) Faith and politics for Arab Christians

Christian and Muslim Arabs should meet in order to reflect together upon *the role of Arab Christians and their calling in the Arab world and beyond*.

c) Lebanon

The Islamic Conference of Jeddah, the World Muslim League, the World Muslim Congress, the WCC and the Vatican should invite 30 Lebanese men and women, 15 Muslims and 15 Christians, to a conference in Geneva (or elsewhere in Europe) to discuss *the problems of reconciliation, peace and justice in Lebanon.* Half of the participants would be selected from among those who took part in the fighting. The conference should not be publicized in advance. [1]

d) Muslims in Europe

The WCC and the Vatican should encourage the Conference of European Churches, the European Conference of Catholic Bishops and the Islamic Council of Europe to bring together *Christians to meet settled and migrant Muslims in Europe* in order to discuss matters of mutual concern.

e) Developing countries

Especially in Asian and African developing countries Christians and Muslims should *discuss together the conception and construction of a community based on social justice and integral human development.* They should together initiate and administer projects for the benefit of all their neighbours; in order to do this, they will need to find ways to *share resources and work together* and thereby to foster a just and participatory society.

f) Christians and Muslims in situations of political tension

Consideration should be given to forming *joint delegations of Muslims and Christians to visit areas of Christian-Muslim tension* to analyze the experiences of these situations and to share hopes for reconciliation.

D. Theology and dialogue

1. Adherents of living faiths in dialogue with one another need to attempt not only to come to as clear an understanding as possible of traditional, credal and confessional statements of members of the respective faiths, but also to clarify together the ways in which reflection on creed can be set in the context of contemporary social and political concerns.

---

[1] A preliminary meeting of about 12 Muslims and 12 Christians from Lebanon (plus some Druse participants) took place in Geneva in June 1977. Participants were welcomed by representatives of the WCC and Sodepax.

a) Revelation

The Qur'an itself offers the basis for a rich understanding of revelation. Christians believe that God has revealed himself in Jesus Christ — his life, death and resurrection; they also recognize God's work in nature — the continuing work of the Holy Spirit and his guidance through prophetic individuals and in history.

For some Christians and for some Muslims, humanity's changing and varying responses to revelation constitute the dynamic consciousness of revelation in contrast to a more static approach which regards the human response to revelation as fixed and takes one or another traditional response as valid for all times.

There may also be a restatement of revelation alongside another revelation according to the pattern of the human challenges that change from one generation to another. Human reflection and obedience, even though they are based on faith, are an ambivalent complex, affected as they are by social and cultural structures.

b) Inter-religious attitudes

It was noted that there is need for Christians and Muslims to consider the significance of one to the other. Within Islam there is place for the "People of the Book". What theological significance does Christianity give to Islam? There are resources within the Bible and Christian tradition to continue to answer this question. Today both Christians and Muslims need to ask afresh what is the religious significance of the one for the other in relation to:

i) increasing interdependence of human communities;

ii) recognition of common human problems; and

iii) common responsibility for the future.

c) Faith, science, technology and the future of humanity

It was in the context of the common responsibility for the future that the question of the relationship of technology and revelation was taken up as technology constituted the common ecology for all religious communities. It was agreed that the role of religion vis-à-vis technology, industrial culture, alienation, and the destructive implications of technological power be allowed to figure on the agenda of future dialogues.

d) Christian mission and Islamic da'wah

Christian mission and Islamic *da'wah* are integral to our respective faiths. We should seek to purify our motives and methods in the practice of mission and *da'wah* and should avoid exploiting the weakness of others.

2. On the basis of these observations, the following items were proposed for future discussions between Christians and Muslims:

a) Revelation

Revelation could be a theme for numerous study projects which might prepare material and participants for a future international dialogue. Particular groups might take up such subjects as:

i) What are the ways in which Christians and Muslims understand the givenness of revelation today?

ii) How do we as persons of faith relate our given understanding of revelation to our life of prayer and obedience?

iii) Relationships between revelation, revolution and revival.

iv) The way in which a religious minority or a dominant religious majority will use a scripture.

v) What is the relevance of revelation for social reconstruction in relation to problems of poverty, disease, suffering and injustice?

vi) Does history challenge us to a comparative approach to revelation?

b) Inter-religious attitudes

Groups of *theologically trained Christians and Muslims could meet to examine the issue of the resources of their respective theological traditions to address the needs of the religiously pluralist situations.* Special attention should be given to *answering the questions of young people who grow up in pluralist societies* and who react against an apparent divisiveness in religions.

c) Faith, science, technology and the future of humanity

This could be the subject for a forthcoming *dialogue between Christian and Muslim theologians, sociologists, natural scientists etc.* This theme could contribute helpfully to the parallel conversations being undertaken with the adherents of other world religions. Many of our secular neighbours could also appreciate the finding of such a dialogue concerning God-given human responsibility in a world scarred by the ecological crises, ethical dilemmas and social problems which have been accentuated by modern science and technology but as yet have been insufficiently answered by people of living faiths. [2]

---

[2] It is expected that a small group of Christian and Muslim natural scientists and theologians will meet in Lebanon in November 1977 to embark upon this theme.

d) Christian mission and Islamic da'wah

The October 1976 issue of the International Review of Mission which was based on the June 1976 dialogue at Chambésy *is commended for study by groups of Christians and Muslims.* They should analyze and evaluate the Chambésy statement and, in response to it, should assess the contemporary activities of mission and *da'wah.* In any future studies concerning mission and *da'wah* the historic and the cultural context in which they are practised and the ideological struggles in the world with which they may be involved should be kept in mind.

Participants

Christians

Dr Peter G. Gowing (joint moderator)
Director, Dansalan Research Center
Dansalan College, P.O. Box 5430
Iligan City, 8801, Philippines

Fr Abou Mokh
Pontifical Commission Secretary
for Relations with Islam
Secretariat for Non-Christians
16, p.s. Calisto
Vatican City, Rome, Italy

Dr George Habib Bebawi
19 Hussein Ahmad, Rashad
Dokki, Giza, Egypt

Dr Sam V. Bhajjan
Director, Henry Martyn Institute
of Islamic Studies
P.O. Box 153, Station Road
Hyderabad 500001, India

The Rt Rev. David Brown
Bishop of Guildford
Willow Grange, Woking Road
Guildford, Surrey, England

Mr Joseph Guelly
General Secretary
Sudan Council of Churches
P.O. Box 469, Khartoum, Sudan

Dr Penelope Johnstone
Centre for the Study of Islam and
Christian-Muslim Relations
Selly Oak Colleges
Birmingham B29 6LE
England

Mr Albert Laham
P.O. Box 4361
Beirut, Lebanon

Dr Lamin Sanneh
Department for the Study of Religions
University of Ghana
P.O. Box 66
Legon, Accra, Ghana

Dr Jane Smith
Acting Director, Center for the
Study of World Religions
Harvard University
42 Francis Avenue
Cambridge, MA, USA

Dr Antonie Wessels
Leidsestraatweg 11
Oegstgeest, Netherlands

Fr Dr Youssef Abdou Youssef
4 Ahmed Heshmat Street
Zamalek, Cairo, Egypt

Muslims

Dr Harun Nasution (joint moderator)
Rektor IAIN — Jakarta
Jalan Ciputat Raya
Kebayoran Lama
Jakarta, Indonesia

Mr Ahmed Ould Abdullah
Head of the Information Department
Organization of the Islamic
Conference of Jeddah
Saudi Arabia

Dr Musa O.A. Abdul
Department of Arabic
and Islamic Studies
University of Ibadan
Ibadan, Nigeria

Prof. Khurshid Ahmad
Director-General
The Islamic Foundation
223 London Road
Leicester LE2 1ZE, England

Prof. Mohammed Arkoun
3 place de l'Etoile
91210 Draveil, France

Dr Hasan Askari
Head, Department of Sociology
Aligarh Muslim University
Aligarh, UP, India

Mr Yahya Basalamah
2 rue Grange-Lévrier
1220 Avanchet-Parc
Geneva, Switzerland

Shaykh Mahmud Bouzouzou
9 rue Royaume
1207 Geneva, Switzerland

Mr Nagib El-Rawi
14 rue Robert de Traz
1206 Geneva, Switzerland

Dr Abdullah El-Tayib
c/o Arabic Department
Faculty of Arts
University of Khartoum
Khartoum, Sudan

Dr Ezzeddin Ibrahim
Cultural Adviser
Presidential Court
Abu Dhabi, United Arab Emirates

Dr Hassan Saab
Ibn Roshd Street
Zaidania, Beirut

WCC staff and interpreters

Dr Philip Potter
General Secretary
World Council of Churches
P.O. Box 66
1211 Geneva 20, Switzerland

Mrs Tomoko Evdokimoff
Language Department
World Council of Churches

Mrs Nicole Fischer
Interpreter
c/o World Council of Churches

Rev. Jean-Marie Lambert
Africa Desk, Commission on
Inter-Church Aid, Refugee
and World Service
World Council of Churches

Pastor Mobbs
3 avenue Grenade
1207 Geneva, Switzerland

Miss Noella Mochizuki
Secretary, World Council of Churches

Dr Constantin Patelos
Faith and Order
World Council of Churches

Dr Stanley Samartha
Director, Dialogue with People
of Living Faiths and Ideologies
World Council of Churches

Miss Irene Smith
Interpreter/Secretary
World Council of Churches

Dr John B. Taylor
Christian-Muslim Relations
Dialogue with People of
Living Faiths and Ideologies
World Council of Churches

Fr George Tsetsis
Middle East Desk
Commission on Inter-Church Aid,
Refugee and World Service
World Council of Churches

Dr Franz von Hammerstein
Christian-Jewish relations
Dialogue with People of
Living Faiths and Ideologies
World Council of Churches

Apologies

Mrs Nisa Ali
19 Central Park Road
London E6 3DZ, England

Mr Gabriel Habib
Assistant General Secretary
Executive Secretary, Department
on Information and Interpretation
Middle East Council of Churches
Unit on Service, P.O. Box 4047
Nicosia, Cyprus

Dr Paul Löffler
Kantstrasse 1
D-6072 Dreieichenhain
Federal Republic of Germany

Dr Seyyed Hossein Nasr
Director, Imperial Iranian Academy
of Philosophy
No. 6 Kouche Nezami
Avenue Faranseh
P.O. Box 14/1699
Tehran, Iran

Bishop Samuel
Bishop of Public, Ecumenical
and Social Services
Coptic Orthodox Church
Anba Rueis Building, Ramses Street
. Abbasiya, Cairo, Egypt

Bishop J. Victor Samuel
113 Qasim Road
Multan, Pakistan

II. 3
"Faith, Science and Technology and the Future of Humanity"

This summary account is not a formal minutes of proceedings. Each day's events were summarized by a Christian and a Muslim participant working together and their summary was shared with the group. It was hoped that the issues and questions raised would provoke an agenda for further such discussions in local situations.

First theme: historical and conceptual analysis

Members of the consultation between Christians and Muslims on "Faith, Science and Technology and the Future of Humanity" had their first formal meeting on Tuesday, 15 November 1977.

The moderator, Dr D.C. Mulder, welcomed the participants and stressed the importance of identifying certain fundamental areas of agreement and promoting cooperation between the two large religious communities, Christian and Muslim, for the better use of science and technology for the future of humanity.

Dr W.C. Smith then presented his paper, "A historian looks at faith, science and technology", on the main theme of the consultation in which he included the following points (the text of Dr Smith's paper is available from WCC):

a) The encompassing view of history as including everything except God who is both within and beyond history.

b) Science should be understood as one aspect of human activity with its grandeur and limits.

c) Modern science can be based on an insight that is true but expressed in a statement that is false.

d) Science is human, finite and always in process, thus it is not the Truth.

e) The Truth is God, and God is not a pattern. His Truth is not propositional.

In the ensuing discussion the participants had, among others, the following points to make:

a) Faith and science can be seen on two levels, the abstract and the social. At the abstract level, science has its own logic and is a way of approaching the truth. Faith comes from God, and so is outside the scientific logic, thus there should be no contradiction between faith and science.

b) Does revelation occur within history or outside history?

c) Does history mediate revelation and does it stand under judgment?

d) How can we know God through history if God is beyond history?

e) Revelation always happens to persons. It occurs daily in the life of believers through the Holy Book and in other ways.

f) No one's knowledge of God is perfect and no reception of revelation is total. Understanding of any religion is less than adequate.

g) There is a distinction between knowing and saying. We all have "known" transcendence, but when we put it into words this becomes historically conditioned.

h) There is also a distinction between articulate and inarticulate knowledge. In science the gap between the two is small whereas in faith it is large.

i) If all expressions of religious truth were relative could there be ethical values which are absolute in themselves?

j) Is the concreteness or fixedness of religious traditions inherent in the scriptures or does it lie in the minds of the believers?

k) Has humanity's role changed from guardian of the land to its salesman? Is this a legitimate interpretation or a degeneration of the biblical and Qur'anic view of humanity's relationship to nature?

l) What do other religious traditions like Hinduism have to teach us in this regard?

m) Our understanding of our place in nature influences our behaviour. What is the role of religion in creating the necessary consciousness of harmony between humanity and nature?

n) To what extent is our future conditioned by our own actions and to what extent is it conditioned by God's will? Are we working out the destruction of God's world, or is it just part of humanity's arrogant claim for itself?

Second theme: ecological and socio-political concerns

1. Ecological concerns

The Friday session began with remarks of Dr Qureshi on the paper of Dr Attiyah "The humanization of technology: a view on a threshold of realignment" (available from WCC, Geneva). Dr Qureshi shared the view expressed in the paper concerning pollution as a rate rather than a quantity. The consideration that the dissipation process was adequate was not acceptable as such to Dr Qureshi.

The dangers for humanity of technological over-development were first discussed. These are of a physical and a spiritual nature. After some discussions it was agreed that:

a) the physical effects do not yet constitute irreversible doom;

b) in the relatively short time that these effects have been recognized a wide awareness has grown, considerable research has been done and many regulations have been made by governments of industrialized nations;

c) there is a need for continued education and research in this field;

d) sustainable technology, fitting to each area, should be developed rather than blindly repeating the mistakes of the Western nations elsewhere.

The energy crisis was also discussed. It was agreed that:

a) what is an oil crisis in the West can be a wood crisis (with consequent problems of erosion) in the East and may lead to food shortage (lack of fertilizers) in certain Eastern countries;

b) these are problems of great complexity with a worldwide inter-relatedness, requiring both local research and internationally agreed solutions; hence Christian-Muslim cooperation can be very important;

c) there is a need for the development of alternative energy sources, again adapted to the local situation, and for economizing on the use of energy, especially in the "rich" nations;

d) similar statements can be made concerning the exhaustion of other raw materials.

2. Socio-political concerns

Dr H. Askari was asked to initiate discussion on the socio-political aspects of the subject. He made the distinction between science as a method and science as a world-view, between technology as an instrument and technology as a system. Then he referred to the modern city as a creation of modern technology and science creating the new school (new educational techniques, methods and values).

Reference was also made to the modern state and its use of science and technology. The question of social and economic justice was also raised since science and technology could be used by oppressive and exploiting groups in an unjust social order.

The spiritual and moral aspects of technological over-development were discussed in connection with the socio-political aspects. The subject was introduced by Dr Askari, who stressed three consequences of the scientific-technological advances in our society:

a) They have brought forth a new school (divorce between science and faith), a new family (the nuclear, privatized family), a new city (slums, alienation), a new distribution system (impersonal super-markets versus small shops, and communal markets), and a new communication pattern.

b) They have greatly affected the state (democratic governments become less democratic because the decisions are too complex for effective parliamentary control; non-democratic governments become more repressive, e.g. through possession of sophisticated arms; in Islamic countries moreover an intervening institution as the church is lacking).

c) The paradoxical situation that science, which promised freedom from superstition, has become a cult of its own (scientism), whereas technology, which promised freedom from want, has actually taken away freedom.

The state controls science and technology with all the dangers for human freedom.

The third world welcomes the material promises of modern technology, but is confused about the values (or lack of values) inherent in it. The Marxist looks only at the socio-economic aspects of technology, but neglects the moral consequences.

We, as Muslims and Christians, should concern ourselves also with the moral aspects of technological development; we should raise the question of what we are doing and even dare to call a stop to those developments that are detrimental to social justice and spiritual wellbeing of our peoples.

In the discussion some recommendations were formulated:

a) Development work should be directed to let a community reach a minimum level, but not go beyond a maximum level, of economic wellbeing so as to enable individuals and communities to cultivate moral and spiritual values.

b) The two religious communities should develop, where possible in cooperation, educational material and programmes on various levels (religious teachers, adult members and young people), which:

— should help to relate the religious insights to the modern scientific insights;
— should help to bring the psychological, ecological and social as technological development into focus (cf. WCC Church and Society programme "Energy for my Neighbour").

c) The two religious communities should cooperate in establishing pilot projects of sustainable technological development, in which local population as well as young Muslim and Christian volunteers from "advanced" countries could be involved.

Furthermore, the following emphases were brought out in the discussion:

a) A common set of formulations may not be adequate to describe the crisis of the rich and the crisis of the poor.
b) While the demographic factors could be associated with the crisis of the poor, it has been the resources crisis which has provoked the crisis of the rich.
c) Is the question of science and technology "a question between scientists" only? Or is it to be shared in discussion by religious groups and by others in the communities?
d) What are the values that are characteristic of development?
e) The word "development" was considered to confuse matters more than clarify them. The very question of assuming economic development as development should be reformulated, and a more integrated view of development be offered.
f) The modes of exploitation between communities have varied in history. The scientific and technological resources could be used for exploitative and destructive ends. Hence, the great and urgent need to emphasize the question of relationship between Christians and Muslims where socio-economic and rural behaviour seem deeply to affect the coming human history.

Third theme: theological concerns

The Thursday session again opened with readings from the Bible and the Qur'an, followed by a short period of silent meditation. Because of the indisposition of Dr Mulder, Dr Askari acted as chairman.

Dr Bonting introduced his own paper "Creation viewed by theology and science: attempt at a synthesis" (available from WCC, Geneva). He also summarized the paper of G.M. Teutsch on "Man's responsibility for the created world, according to (the) Christian view", also earlier distributed (available from WCC, Geneva).

The discussion that followed was intense. Various themes may be seen as having been pursued, with several aspects of each being tackled.

a) Humanity's relation to nature

It was observed that in both the Islamic and the Christian cases humanity's relation to God (and to fellow humans) has traditionally been considered a good deal more centrally than has humanity's relation to nature. Recently, this last has been treated by science; the need for faith to accept, to supplement, or to correct this treatment was canvassed.

The synthesis put forth in Dr Bonting's paper of the scientific presentation of evolution with the biblical presentation of creation was discussed at length. A relative lack of comparable problems felt in the case of the Qur'an was remarked, but in both cases present-day anti-synthesis moods, or hesitations, were noted and considered. Some suggested that the long-range process of evolution has entered a new phase in recent human history, at least in human consciousness, especially with the rapid transformations engendered in and through science and technology.

Not only the new sense of power, for both good and evil (Hiroshima), but also a sense of helplessness before the very forces of science and technology, were remarked. The theological implications discerned in this varied. A Christian's phrasing of humanity perceived now as co-worker with God in human history struck Muslim ears as perilously close to the sin of *shirk*. There was discussion too as to where history is headed: to a divine consummation, to a Day of Judgment, to a goal controlled by God, by humanity, or by aimless chance.

b) The role of Jesus Christ as seen by Christians and Muslims

A second theme was the place of Jesus Christ in human history and in cosmic evolution. Christians present were moved at Muslim insistence that this question be taken seriously, and the suggestion that so long as doctrinal formulations were not stressed Christ could become an important symbol for Muslims too (as indeed he is in the Qur'an), as humanity wrestles with the deepest problems of science, technology, and its own future.

The symbol of the cross, its meaning for Muslims and for Christians, the role of suffering and of willingness to suffer, of potential defeat and ultimate victory for persons as they plunge into the present crisis, received considerable attention. Also the question was addressed of the connotations of the cross for not only person but city, for society and social justice.

While Muslims spoke of the potential significance of the Christ figure for their community, Christians spoke of the Qur'an as a reminder to them of universal social covenant, of corporate justice and racial equality. Members of both communities were moved by the deep expressions of mutual involvement and genuine "thank you's".

c) The spiritual significance of our meeting's taking place in Lebanon

The stark situation in Lebanon where the group was meeting was impressed on all participants. Between the heights of true faith and its ability to know God — including knowing him as God "of both sides" — and the depths of the recent warfare and its atrocities, the vivid gap was recognized. Two needs were stressed. One was to study more carefully, to recognize and make known more truly, the actual sociological facts of religious life "as lived", the play upon it of outside forces, and of violence, and the use of religious symbols for group fanaticisms. The other was to lift up from each tradition neither creeds that formalize and divide nor yet degenerated symbols used for crass purposes but rather central faith motifs, such as "redemption" in the Christian sense and *istighfar*, the humility that seeks forgiveness, in the Islamic; in the conviction that true faith, in each case, as expressed in such motifs, could (alone) heal the sorrows of a torn society, and enable humanity to deal with the formidable problems and potentialities that science and technology proffer. It was also noted that social justice, as a goal of true faith in each case, may have to precede, or at least to accompany, mutual understanding.

II. 4
Christians and Muslims Living Together

IN THE NAME OF GOD

The Christian and Muslim participants in the planning meeting held in Chambésy, 12-14 March 1979, at the invitation of the World Council of Churches, reviewed the principles and suggestions from previous Christian-Muslim meetings under various auspices. They faced again the continuing tensions between communities but were able to issue this commonly prepared and agreed report. They reaffirmed some principles and proposed future plans for improving Christian-Muslim understanding and relations. The working out of these principles and proposals could constitute a shared programme or process on the theme "Christians and Muslims Living Together".

I. Some principles for Christian-Muslim relations

1. Christians and Muslims live together in an increasingly pluralistic and interdependent world. Living together brings blessings but also problems; pluralism can be a dynamic and enriching process but it can also be intrusive and destabilizing. We therefore have a spiritual and moral duty to relate to each other in mutual respect for each other's religious convictions and commitments. As part of humanity, we accept a common God-given responsibility to work for peace and justice.

2. We should take account of the variety of situations in which Muslims and Christians live. There is no common pattern in relations between Christians and Muslims in different parts of the world. We expect people in each given situation to set the pace and choose the style

for their own involvement in talking and working together. Nevertheless, we recognize the extent to which we have often shared a common history and may share an increasingly common future.

3. We should draw upon the riches of the scriptures, doctrines and traditions of both Muslims and Christians in promoting good relationships with each other. We should also be aware of the non-doctrinal factors which affect our relationships; social, political, ethnic, ideological and cultural factors may divide us or unite us.

4. We should be aware of the suspicions which still surround dialogue in the minds of some Christians and Muslims. The process of dialogue calls for patience, generosity and courage; we should never appear to be imposing the claims of dialogue. Nevertheless, we recognize the necessity for consultation and cooperation in order to ease tensions, for example concerned with human rights. We must strive to overcome stereotypes and bias; we must try to overcome ignorance, misunderstandings and the falsifications and caricatures of each other's faith which appear in the mass media, textbooks, etc.

5. We welcome dialogue between Muslims and Christians as a mood, a spirit and an attitude which may appear new but which are in fact integral to the teachings and history of our respective faiths. Dialogue is a readiness to learn as well as to share information, to receive as well as to give.

6. Building upon this attitude and readiness Christians and Muslims may undertake deliberate meetings for dialogue but may also undertake concrete projects cooperatively and in mutual respect.

7. We respect a vocation for dialogue as one among many vocations which may contribute to improving Christian-Muslim understanding and relations. However we recognize that dialogue may also be abused and exploited. We therefore insist that dialogue must never be used as a tool for proselytism.

8. Organized missionary activities generate tensions between Christians and Muslims and are causing increasing concern. In order to build trust and confidence and for the sake of future relations between us these activities should be restrained. However, proper understanding of each other's beliefs, teaching and attitudes should be facilitated.

9. We should welcome and stimulate the enthusiasm about improving understanding and relations such as is often shown by some of the younger generation. For some people dialogue can be part of their own spiritual experience and self-awareness. A deliberate effort should be

made to encourage and enable young Christians and young Muslims to meet each other.

10. We see the importance of involving in dialogue all the various levels — official, popular and academic — in both our communities. Particular efforts should be made to engage both those organizations and individuals with special interest and experience of Christian-Muslim relations and those men and women, young and old, with appropriate qualifications who command the trust of their own community. We recognize that different criteria for involvement will be used depending upon whether it is a mainly consultative or mainly representative meeting or project. We should be sensitive to the provision of translation and interpretation facilities.

11. We desire to avoid all confusion and syncretism which may come from attempts to worship together. We may however expect to invoke God's blessing on all we undertake together and to listen together to our respective scripture.

12. We desire that all planning should continue to be undertaken jointly by both partners.

II. Proposed plans for the future

The Christian and Muslim participants in the planning meeting propose to their respective communities that the following possibilities be taken up during the next two to three years, always with an eye to longer term developments. It is not expected that all of these suggestions can be realized in so relatively short a time, but it is hoped that various Christian and Islamic organizations at international, regional and local levels may select and possibly reformulate one or more of the proposed items for their individual sponsorship or for sponsorship together with another organization. Together these suggestions could comprise a programme on "Christians and Muslims Living Together".

1979 Phase I: Preparation within our respective communities
a) Correspondence with and reports and visits to bodies represented at or invited to the planning meeting, to other interested bodies and to individuals.
b) Possible meeting among Christians to discuss relations with Muslims under the auspices of the World Council of Churches in cooperation with the Vatican.
c) Possible meeting among Muslims to discuss relations with Christians under the auspices of an Islamic organization.

d) Possible meetings or study programmes on Christian-Muslim relations under the auspices of cultural organizations or academic institutions.

1979-81 Phase II: Joint programme and projects shared by Muslims and Christians
a) An exchange of basic information
— "The Islamic State and Human Brotherhood" — a seminar possibly under the auspices of an Islamic organization or institution.
— "Christian Arabs and Muslim Arabs Living Together" — a conversation possibly under the auspices of the Middle East Council of Churches. Other regional conferences might be undertaken under the auspices of Christian and/or Muslim organizations.
— "The Concern for Religious Education" — a seminar possibly jointly organized by Islamic and Christian bodies (including educationalists).
— "Values of Family Life in Cultural Perspective" — a seminar possibly under the auspices of an international women's organization in consultation with Islamic and Christian bodies.
— "Islamic and Christian Aspirations for Jerusalem" — a colloquium possibly under the auspices of the Organization of the Islamic Conference.

b) Cooperation in shared concerns
— Meeting of Christians and Muslims engaged in teaching subjects related to Islam and Christianity (with particular attention to the issues of textbooks and training programmes) possibly under the auspices of the Centre for the Study of Islam and Christian-Muslim Relations, Selly Oak Colleges, Birmingham, in cooperation with institutions and study centres in Asia, Africa, etc. and taking account of the work of Unesco, etc.
— "Common Concerns for Human Rights" — correspondence, documentation and colloquium possibly under the auspices of the Islam and the West Programme.
— Youth Conference on "Faith and Spirituality in the Modern World", possibly under the auspices of an Islamic or Christian youth or students' organization or jointly undertaken by such organizations.
— Discussion about "The Ethics and Practices of Economic Aid Programmes and Humanitarian Assistance" possibly under the auspices of a secular aid agency or development studies programme.

— "Sharing of Experiences and Ethical Aspirations in Relation to Innovative Banking Systems" — a colloquium possibly under the auspices of an Islamic and/or Christian organization.
— Follow-up of international WCC conference on "Faith, Science and the Future", July 1979 (in which both Christians and Muslims will participate) possibly under the joint auspices of Christian and Islamic organizations.

c) Preparatory meeting for an international Muslim-Christian conference including participants from Islamic and Christian organizations.

1980-81 Phase III: International conference on "Christians and Muslims Living Together" jointly sponsored by Islamic and Christian organizations — possibly part of the celebrations to mark the opening years of the 15th century of the hijrah. Such a conference should build on previous activities and stimulate further such activities.

Participants

Muslims

Dr Ezzeddin Ibrahim
(representing the Organization
of the Islamic Conference)
Presidential Court
Abu Dhabi, United Arab Emirates

Dr Muhammad Rasjidi
(representing the World Muslim
Congress)
Jalan Diponegoro 42
Jakarta, Indonesia

Dr Mushirul Haq
Mushir Manzil, Jamia Nagar
New Delhi 110025, India

Dr Harun Nasution
IAIN Syarif Hidayatullah
Jalan Ciputat Raya, Kebayoran Lama
Jakarta-Selatan, Indonesia

Prof. Dr Mohammed Talbi
11 rue de Téhéran
Le Bardo, Tunis, Tunisia

Replies and apologies received from:

World Muslim League, Mecca
Al-Azhar University, Cairo
Institute of Muslim Minority Affairs,
   Jiddah

Christians

Dr T.B. Simatupang
(one of the Presidents of the WCC)
Jalan Diponegoro 55
Jakarta, Indonesia

Dr D.C. Mulder
(moderator of the Working Group of
the programme of DFI, WCC)
108 Jacob Marisstraat
Amsterdam, Netherlands

Père Michel Lelong
(representing the Vatican Secretariat
for Non-Christians)
34 avenue Reille
75014 Paris, France

Dr Marcel Boisard
(joint commissioner, Islam and the West Programme)
Case postale 53
1211 Geneva 21, Switzerland

Mr Gabriel Habib
Middle East Council of Churches
P.O. Box 5376, Beirut, Lebanon
(substituted on 12 March by
Mr Albert Latham
62 quai Gustave Ador
Geneva, Switzerland)

Dr David Kerr
Selly Oak Colleges
Birmingham B29 6LE
United Kingdom

Bishop Johnson Komora
(nominated by Islam in Africa Project)
Kingsmead College
Selly Oak Colleges
Birmingham B29 6LE
United Kingdom

Apologies received from:

Dr Peter Gowing
Dansalan Research Centre
Marawi City, Philippines

His Excellency Bethuel Kiplagat
High Commissioner of Kenya, Paris

WCC staff

Dr S.J. Samartha
Dr J.B. Taylor
Mrs J. Spechter

II. 5
Living as Faithful People in a Changing Society

The first day of summer 1980 saw the opening of the first Muslim-Christian youth dialogue at the Ecumenical Institute at the Château de Bossey, 25 kms north of Geneva. Our group of almost fifty men and women, most of whom ranged in age from 20 to 35, but some of whom were older, came from the Middle East, Asia, Africa, Latin America, North America, the Pacific Islands and Europe. We gathered together for a week of study, dialogue and fellowship. Although the weather was cooler and wetter than most had anticipated, spirits were high and the atmosphere was one of openness and great warmth. Daily prayers at noon for Muslims and morning devotions for Christians enriched and intensified our engagements. Our emphasis on the future provided an opportunity for the hope and optimism of some to be multiplied and shared by all.

Our needs were more than fully met by the Bossey staff who not only looked after our hospitality but also participated in some of our sessions, displaying keen interest and numerous talents.

At first we faced some difficulties in our endeavours at understanding exactly what each one of us wanted to say, first of all in plenary introductions and then in groups. But, as our social evening made very clear, we were quickly growing together as friends. That evening of wonderful fellowship and laughter certainly helped us to return to our group discussions with renewed vigour.

We were also helped by the peaceful environment at Bossey and by the very friendly staff. The walks to and from the buildings made us appreciate God's creation; surrounded by tall trees and green grass we felt refreshed in mind and body.

An occasion which none present will forget was the trip to John Mott House, the World Council of Churches, and the mosque in Geneva, followed by the reception at John and Margaret Taylor's home; this trip added materially to our fellowship and understanding of each other.

In the last 24 hours we presented to each other the reports of our three groups. These were welcomed as a basis of continuing reflection amongst ourselves and a possible basis for further discussion with Christian and Muslim friends in our home countries. We ended our meeting with a simple act of listening to passages of each other's scriptures and of exchanging the greeting "The peace of God be upon you".

Group report 1: Faith and religious tradition as promoters of change

A spirit of peace and mutual attentiveness, of fellowship and friend-ship, marked the discussions in this group. Throughout its two days' work, respect for the partner and a concern that the debate should be conducted at the level of persons prevailed.

People from the following countries shared in the work of this group: Egypt, France, Greece, Lebanon, Spain, Syria, Turkey, USA, USSR and West Germany.

Discussion focused on such topics as: separation of state and religion; Muslims and Christians of the third world/of the West; faith and religion; individual faith and open-ended change in society; return to the sources: hope/danger; faith and the struggle against masked idols; being a minority, alone, not isolated; divine support; balance between the material and the spiritual; new economic order; language problems (e.g. light, darkness, justice, etc.); witness of Muslims and Christians living in Europe; witness of Christians living or having lived in Muslim countries; Muslims and Christians who tend to have a "superiority complex" not only in relation to each other but also towards others.

Can faith and religious tradition promote changes?

Our answer to this question is "yes", if the distinction between faith and religion is respected. This reservation is absolutely essential when reference is made to the need for a return to the sources and when it is noted that dangers and hopes go together. Said one member of the group: "I have been moved by our agreement that we need to return to the original traditions and purify them from all impurities, misunderstand-ings..." If the turn to the sources promotes change, it is recognized that this change must, above all, take place in each one of us. The group stressed the need for "an inner change in our faith as personal relationship with God". This is the sense of the formula "the God of the now". In the group's opinion, this constant relationship with a living God can help to avert or reduce the anticipated dangers of the return to the sources. We agree that all believers should engage personally at the heart of their own faith in a struggle against what we call "the masked idols". In this struggle we can all of us find ourselves alone, confronted with our individual responsibilities and watched by two witnesses: our conscience and God.

At this level the sense of being a minority is relativized by the fact that, when we respond justly to the appeal of a just and loving God, we are all of us in this position. "The sense of being a minority is exclusively social and political. When we believe, we are neither a minority nor a majority, but human beings before God." In such moments the only thing that matters is the support of God. Solidarity with our brothers and sisters in faith follows, but not before the following task has been accomplished: "Muslims and Christians condemn the polemics they indulged in in the past and the narrow slogans... so as to become open to the mystery of God and to the practice of human freedom in face of the demonic forces of the idols. Likewise, they now abandon all kinds of proselytism which take the aggressive way of denigration or material inducements in order to unsettle ordinary people and turn them away from the faith of their forbears and convert them to another religion."

We were thus invited to "accept diversity, pluralism and differences as an enrichment and not as divisive factors". Moreover, as one woman participant said: "I feel that in order to respect the other person, engage in dialogue together, and to change the present situation, it is essential to see that person secure in his or her faith. It is on this basis that we will be able to accept the other persons as they are, without requiring that they should resemble us." This encounter in the one yet differentiated faith made it possible for one member of our group to make the following testimony: "And I feel that here in Bossey we are beginning to build this new world." He then quoted John 3:7: "You must be born anew", and added: "I have been born again." Someone else had the same feeling: "I know who each of you are — and you are now written in my heart — please keep me in yours." This strongly believing and committed friendship emerges as one of the outstanding fruits produced by this meeting.

This same friendship enabled us to listen sympathetically and responsibly when we came to discuss the problems of Christians and Muslims living as minorities in Islamic or in Christian lands: "Christians or Muslims living as a minority should show tolerance and faith and deepen their relations with the majority of people living in the country." It also encouraged us on both sides to say how our experiences with each other as Christians and Muslims can mutually reinforce us, support us and enlighten us. It is here that we have to affirm, despite the respect that we have for our respective doctrines, that the fellowship encouraged and established by God surpasses all our understanding even as it takes root in our hearts.

Starting from this inner dimension, ceaselessly enlarged and nourished by God, we can all of us envisage change in our societies in the direction of openness. The first difficulty is this: "From a practical standpoint, it is difficult to separate state concerns from religious concerns... Religious concerns are our strongest concern, regardless of whether it is called secular or spiritual. It is the catalyst by which we act. The whole of life is to be approached religiously... But rather I am in quest of a workable solution." The following comment points in the same direction: "Religion in the state is fine, but only if all religions are equal and free." Another group member spoke of his experience "that the separation of religion from state is the main condition for religious freedom". Finally the following statement: "At the temporal level, Muslims and Christians acknowledge all that is positive in their past coexistence. Beyond this, they are seeking a new sense of the Islamic community or of the community of the Christian church, as a deeper form of human communion, limiting and correcting national loyalties and working for peace. They also declare their intention to live together within pluralist states as equals on the basis of their common citizenship, in the spirit of Islam and of Christianity. And by loyalty to the demands for justice and the struggles for justice on both sides, they share in the struggle for justice undertaken by the most marginalized peoples of the earth."

While it is true that we do not live by bread alone, it is also true that we need bread in order to live. At the level of solidarity in the cause of justice as well as for such meetings as this, it is desirable that the initiative should come from both sides.

Group report 2: The ambiguities of cultural dominance

The group working on this theme was made up of representatives from Bangladesh, Egypt, France, India, Malaysia, Netherlands, Nigeria, Pakistan, Syria, Tunisia, Turkey, West Germany, United Kingdom and USA.

Each person described briefly what the ambiguity of cultural dominance meant in his or her own situation. These experiences ranged through a variety of forms of dominance in the cultural, economic, political and religious spheres, and emphasized the devastating effects of imported models of development and "civilization" on a society. We recognized how important is the choice of words in the pursuit of fruitful dialogue.

For example, the term "indigenization" strongly provoked the group. The meanings attached to this term differed radically depending on whether it was used by a Westerner or heard by someone from the third world. A terminology with colonialist overtones is extremely harmful in a meeting of this kind.

Before trying to reconcile existing religions and cultures, it seemed essential to examine relations between religion and society.

Religion and society

The totalitarian tendency of some adherents of religions, especially the great monotheistic faiths, no longer needs to be demonstrated. Between a religion and a society there is an interaction, therefore, which can even spill over into conflicts.

Sociologically, the environment within which a religion is born can fail to match the culture of another region to which this religion is intended to be transplanted. The different possibilities here can range from outright rejection to accommodation or brutal imposition.

In the case of the three monotheist religions, there is one common element: faith in a unique God... and this faith has a universal dimension.

The important thing, for the Muslim-Christian dialogue in particular, is to see the way in which each religion interprets this faith.

Without entering into too much detail, we need to highlight the significance of this dialogue.

Significance of a Muslim-Christian dialogue

At first sight it seems very artificial to classify contemporary societies according to religious criteria. It is plain from the economic and political realities that Christian and Muslim peoples living in the same region can have the same interests. And other factors also need to be taken into account in planning a dialogue.

The problems of third-world countries cannot be treated in isolation from each other. These countries constitute an altogether real unity over against the rich countries.

Dialogue should be established between those with "full bellies" and those with "empty bellies".

That said, the Muslim society nevertheless believes it has proposals to make in face of these inequalities. Since the scientific and economic expansion and the arms build-up of the Western and socialist world affords no solution, the Muslim world is seeking a new and more just society. It thinks it can discover it in its own values, turning back to certain periods in its history and making good use of its own resources. It is here that Islam finds the indissoluble connection between this world and the world to come.

As far as Christians are concerned, despite examples of attempts to create a more just society on earth, they say that this is impossible because of the imperfections of humanity. Ought this to prevent them from working for a better world? Muslims and Christians in various parts of the world are trying to find positive answers to this question, as the Bossey dialogue indicates.

The political and economic responsibility of the religions
The fact remains that in almost all Muslim and Christian countries today, some adherents of these two religions lend legitimacy to political powers which violate human rights, by supporting such authorities at elections, with material aid and in many other ways. The image of the "depraved God"[1] in whose name an illegitimate ideology is fostered is in this respect indicative.

The political parties, appealing to these two religions, are another example of this... not to mention the heads of state who are sworn into office on one of the two sacred books.

Perspectives and conclusions
The question was legitimately raised as to whether the adherents of Christianity and Islam in their present atttitudes are capable of creating peaceful and just societies. We realized that the dynamics of power within the church and the Ummah are not the most effective channels for bringing about change in society, e.g. the question related to development. Initiatives towards change must come from peoples of all faiths; this means cooperation at grassroots levels and also with all people of good will, whether they are believers or not. An attitude of tolerance and a total avoidance of hidden ulterior motives is required as the basis of such cooperation. This would be brought about by a constant renewal of

---

[1] Maurice Bellet, *Le Dieu pervers*, Editions Desclée de Brouwer, Section "Connivence".

the individual's faith in a God who is just, and by his or her consequent behaviour. Believers have the human duty to see that the values of their religion are not used by the "powers that be" in whatever form they are. It is essential that the dialogue that has been started should be continued, pursued and developed everywhere.

Some suggestions for the future
— There must be a renewal of each individual's personal faith.
— Persons in positions of authority within the church and Ummah should spread the message of tolerance — through their schools, religious institutions, agencies and other channels.
— Children particularly need to be educated on the principles and practice of tolerance and other virtues.
— Dialogue must continue wherever possible and at all times. It should be open and honest and not with "hidden agendas", because openness between people leads to relationships which in turn can work for peace and justice in the world.

In our discussion of problems facing societies today, special attention was given to socio-political and economic problems as they affect young people and the rural communities. Reference was made to the refugee situations, the growing gap between the rich and the poor, drug addiction, violence, criminality, loss of community, etc. etc.

Finally
Christians and Muslims should do their best so that religion is not used as a tool by those in power.
— More meetings of this nature should be held frequently.
— A necessary part of the follow-up project should be that joint programmes should be undertaken by participants to continue the dialogue at local levels.

Group report 3: Visions for the future
The group accepted the following questions to be the issues for the discussion:
— What are each participant's experiences with a Muslim-Christian dialogue?
— What are the motives for and the objectives of a Muslim-Christian dialogue?
— What are the barriers between us?

— Does a "secular state" guarantee human rights more so than a state with a religious basis?

— What are our visions as young people of the future?

In the first session each participant related his or her experience with attempts at Christian-Muslim dialogue within their respective regional areas. The group fortunately represented a wide variety of countries: Austria, Bangladesh, Cameroon, Egypt, India, Jordan, Lebanon, Mexico, Pakistan, Palestine, Uganda, United Kingdom, USA, West Germany, Western Samoa/New Zealand. With each person's view it became apparent that actual dialogue and interaction between the peoples of both religious traditions improved the quality of their co-existence.

One participant provided the group with a useful categorization of the people involved in dialogue:

— Conservatives — "traditionalists" — who can be rigid in their attitudes and averse to joining in dialogue; unfortunately they are the majority.

— The "indifferent" whose tolerance of dialogue actually stems from an indifferent attitude of irresponsibility.

— The "liberal-minded" people who are willing to participate with people of other traditions in dialogue. They are a minority.

Barriers facing the dialogue were found to stem from ignorance of the religious tradition of others. The strengths were seen as:

a) having sufficient knowledge of the other;

b) education of the people of the cultures involved;

c) personal involvement with people of the other traditions.

The fact that both the religions are an expression of faith calling for worship of God was emphasized. Other positive factors were the need for humanity to combine its efforts to surmount the problems of the world.

Some apprehension and anxiety arose over the deliberate use of dialogue as a method of converting one party to the other's faith. But the group disclaimed such an intention and condemned this attitude as being insincere and an adulteration of dialogue.

The record of missionaries was also raised and was criticized by both Muslims and Christians with the exception of a few reserved opinions; the point was made that religion was sometimes being used as a political tool to aggravate inter-cultural problems. For example, a European Christian missionary could be imposing a European Christian culture on the indigenous culture and producing both Muslims and Christians who were alienated from their own culture and who were incapable of appreciating the problems of their compatriots.

The final session dealt with visions for the future and with what the two religious traditions could provide for the world. The Muslims called upon the Christians for a more active participation in the solution of the world's problems. It was agreed that both Christians and Muslims should stand against the oppression which exists amongst us and both should draw from their faith the strength to struggle for a better world regardless of the hardships encountered. The message of Jesus Christ was for the down-trodden and the oppressed and it is the duty of his followers to stand for the oppressed over against the world. And it is the Muslims' obligation to struggle for the attainment of justice in order to fulfill the human rights of the peoples involved and to provide people with the opportunities for full expression of their faith.

It was agreed that no single model of government is appropriate for the whole world. The wealth of humanity's heritage provides us with several models but, whichever one is chosen, in a particular nation it must address itself to the particular conditions of the nation involved. It should also call upon the people to fulfill their obligations and responsibilities towards the larger community and the world as a whole. Taking the example of the USA, it was agreed that a "secular state system" is no guarantee against racial discrimination or against the abuse of minorities or even of poor majorities.

II. 6
Ethics and Practices of Humanitarian and Development Programmes

At the invitation of the Hon. Minister of Transport and Muslim Affairs of the Republic of Sri Lanka, and through the hospitality of the government of that friendly country, a conference of Muslim-Christian dialogue was convened in Colombo, 30 March-1 April 1982, on the theme "Christians and Muslims Living and Working Together: Ethics and Practices of Humanitarian and Development Programmes".

Initiated and organized cooperatively by the World Muslim Congress, Karachi, and the World Council of Churches, Geneva, the conference was attended by 33 representatives from the Muslim world and 30 from the Christian churches. Messages and observers were sent from the Secretariat for Non-Christians, Vatican City; the Organization of the Islamic Conference, Jeddah; and Unesco, Paris.

Presided over by the Hon. Mohammed Haniffa Mohamed, Minister of Transport and Muslim Affairs of Sri Lanka, together with H.E. Dr Marouf Al Daoualibi, president of the World Muslim Congress, and Dr T.B. Simatupang, one of the presidents of the World Council of Churches, the conference was moderated by Dr Viqar Hamdani, World Muslim Congress representative to the United Nations, New York, and Dr D.C. Mulder, moderator of the World Council of Churches' Dialogue with People of Living Faiths and Ideologies.

Both parties agreed on the need to discuss the conference theme in a world threatened by materialism and loss of faith, and disfigured by injustices and violations of human rights that have been especially destructive in the context of situations of invasions and displacement of peoples. It was recognized that there are still numerous obstacles in the way of fuller cooperation between Christians and Muslims and there was frank discussion of the suspicions promoted by restriction of cultural and religious rights of any peoples whether majorities or minorities. Both sides expressed concern about the abuse of some humanitarian work when force or false persuasion is used for conversion and proselytism.

The Muslim participants emphasized that cooperation deserves to be built on the foundations of removing obstacles and supporting the victims of aggression and persecution. They stressed the need for:

a) unequivocal condemnation of aggression against the people of Palestine, who have been dispossessed from their homeland and are being subjected to oppression and persecution, of the invasion of Afghanistan, and of the persecution of Muslims in different parts of the world especially in the Southern Philippines;

b) sympathetic appreciation of Muslims' commitment to develop their communities and societies on the basis of their faith and law (shari'ah) on the part of their Christian neighbours and other believing communities, as Muslims struggle to establish the Islamic social order in places where they enjoy political sovereignty;

c) implementation of principles agreed upon in earlier dialogues, particularly that at Chambésy in 1976, in order to remove obstacles to Christian-Muslim cooperation.

While sharing many of the preoccupations expressed by the Muslims, the Christian participants, both in plenary addresses and discussions, emphasized their desire that they might work more closely with Muslim neighbours in nation building and in community development. In some places Christians felt that they were not accepted as full citizens by their Muslim neighbours, while in other places Christians acknowledged their responsibility for having left Muslims with analogous feelings. But the major preoccupation of the Christians was not to allow the suspicions or caricatures of the past to disfigure the present and the future. Determined efforts should be undertaken for closer understanding and more effective partnership with their Muslim neighbours.

Recommendations of the conference lay in three major areas:

A. *Recommendations on Christian-Muslim cooperation*

The participants, having discussed issues of "cooperation in relief and rehabilitation" and of "planning and realizing community development", recommended that:

The World Muslim Congress and the World Council of Churches be requested to establish a joint standing committee with a view to:

1) working out the targets, forms and modalities of Muslim-Christian dialogue in a manner that would ensure authentic participation from both communities and lead to better understanding and greater cooperation among them;
2) identifying obstacles to and difficulties in the healthy pursuit of dialogue and cooperation between the two communities, and using their good offices to redress any such obstacles and difficulties;
3) responding to the challenges of development;
4) giving to human existence its transcendent dimension, which is obstructed by all the forms of misunderstanding of faiths, whether these forms are encouraged by materialist ideologies or inspired by a narrowly scientific interpretation of the achievements of science and technology;
5) undertaking everything possible to promote a form of education that situates knowledge in a truly human perspective where faith and knowledge give each other mutual reinforcement and seek inspiration from divine revelation;
6) studying and examining the possibilities of deepening dialogue on practical action to be undertaken in common and with clear and precise conditions laid down by the joint standing committee; these should reflect the notion of development in the context of justice and as a way of full realization of human potential; there should also be examination of the methods to be used for implementing moral and cultural values in the process of development;
7) instituting joint study groups and holding seminars on Muslim and Christian approaches to the solution of major problems jointly faced by them in their search for a just social order; in this respect the joint standing committee is requested to constitute working groups on the problems of "law (shari'ah) and life", "the role of the state", and "human and religious rights", from the Islamic and Christian points of view;
8) trying to bring into the joint standing committee representatives of other international Islamic organizations and the Roman Catholic Church.

B. Recommendations on refugees

The participants discussed the world refugee problem. Because of internal conflicts and the systematic and flagrant violation of human rights in many countries, the number of refugees has dramatically increased in recent years. This trend was noted with grave concern. The living conditions borne by most of these refugees strike at their dignity and rights as human beings. The participants, therefore, recommended that:

1) since work for refugees is a field in which both Christians and Muslims can cooperate fruitfully together, Christian-Muslim cooperation in alleviating the plight of refugees on international, regional and local levels should be developed; further, Christian churches and Muslim organizations should come together to study the causes of the refugee problem as well as methods of preventing it;

2) Christian churches and Muslim organizations should attempt to convince the appropriate authorities to allow refugees to return to their homeland with a guarantee of security of life, property, and fundamental human rights;

3) noting the enormity of the refugee problem and the fact that over three-quarters of the world's refugees are Muslims, the Muslim participants appeal to the Organization of the Islamic Conference (OIC) to establish a unit to deal with all aspects of the refugee problem; such a unit should cooperate with the existing organizations dealing with refugees;

4) services for refugees should not serve as means for conversion or proselytism and should be made available to all without discrimination;

5) Christian churches and Islamic organizations should encourage the peoples and governments of their respective countries to accept refugees, to have sympathy for their plight and to adhere to international conventions governing assistance to refugees and the granting of asylum to them.

C. Recommendations on minorities

The participants came to a deeper awareness of the fact that Christians and Muslims share the same experience in living both as a majority and as a minority. They are convinced that Christians and Muslims can live together in harmony, but recognized that there is a need to overcome the tensions that exist in some countries. The participants agreed that:

1) each religious group should be enabled to live according to the teachings of its faith with the right to perpetuate itself; in order to do this, full freedom of worship should be guaranteed;

2) particularly where Christians and Muslims are both in the minority they should cooperate with each other to obtain and maintain their freedom of worship and practise their religion;

3) there have been and are persistent and serious violations of the fundamental human rights of religious minorities in many countries; these acts and the governments responsible for them were condemned and it was agreed that the joint standing committee should be asked to study instances of discrimination and persecution and to take appropriate action;

4) marriage, divorce and inheritance and charitable trusts are regulated in a specific manner for Muslims and for some Christian confessions and these provisions should be respected; a serious dialogue should be undertaken to find appropriate ways of maintaining or creating legal safeguards in these matters;

5) multi-religious, multi-cultural and multi-linguistic communities offer new methods of living and working together; these need further study.

Conclusion

The experience of the Christian-Muslim dialogue in Colombo, with its frank and open discussion, has fostered a clear understanding of each other and the determination to work together in the interests of peace, justice and humanity, thus exemplifying Muslims' and Christians' united commitment to achieve God's purposes for humanity.

REPORT OF WCC DELEGATION
TO CHRISTIAN-MUSLIM DIALOGUE

In the three days following the Christian-Muslim dialogue, held under the joint auspices of the World Council of Churches and the World Muslim Congress, in Colombo, Sri Lanka, the Christian participants evaluated the meeting and agreed upon the following report:

We, the delegates appointed by the World Council of Churches to participate in the Christian-Muslim dialogue on "Living and Working Together", have met following that dialogue, 3-5 April 1982, in Colombo. After studying the document presenting the final report of the dialogue, we offer the following recommendations to the World Council of Churches and its constituent member churches:

I. Regarding future structure for continuing dialogue, we recommend:

1) that the WCC work towards the establishment of a joint standing committee with the World Muslim Congress (WMC);

2) that in the first phase this committee have the status of a liaison and planning committee;

3) that as soon as possible efforts be made to bring the Roman Catholic Church and other international Islamic organizations into the joint standing committee;
4) that possible membership for the committee be up to twenty, with up to ten on either side, and a limited number of ad hoc advisory observers;
5) that Christian membership of the committee include experts in different fields and be largely made up of people who live in the Muslim world or who work with Muslims.

II. Regarding relief and rehabilitation, we recommend:
1) that the WCC and its constituent member churches reaffirm that diakonia is the expression of God's love to all those in need, regardless of religion or nationality, with no intention of proselytism or benefit to those practising such diakonia, though not hiding that we are Christians;
2) that the WCC, its member churches and related agencies study whether, in certain special circumstances, the provision of resources for relief and rehabilitation should preferably be channelled through other humanitarian organizations;
3) that the churches continue to pay special attention to the task of transforming relief and first-help service into a long-range process of rehabilitation and development and encourage cooperation between Christians, Muslims and other communities in this task.

III. Regarding development, we recommend:
1) that, in the continuation of the dialogue, attention be given at the earliest opportunity to reflection on the challenges of development, and that for this purpose the WCC call upon the special competence of the Commission on the Churches' Participation in Development and its staff;
2) that Christian-Muslim dialogue regarding development be encouraged at the national and local levels, taking into consideration the political, economic and social context within each nation and community;
3) that a study be made of particular development projects in which Christians and Muslims are cooperating, with a view to learning which methods are effective and which are not, and to sharing those models which may be adapted elsewhere;
4) that the WCC and churches in the industrialized countries call upon the governments of the industrialized countries to hear the appeal of

the nations of the South to establish a new international economic order, and to share a larger proportion of their Gross National Product in development assistance to poorer countries, working towards the goal of 0.7% of GNP called for by the United Nations, in order to share in their struggle for justice;

5) that churches around the world be called upon to share a larger proportion of their resources for development programmes in developing countries, with a view to struggling together with the peoples of those nations for a more just, participatory and sustainable global society to the glory of God and the fulfilment of the potential of his creation.

IV. Regarding refugees, we recommend:

1) that the WCC heartily endorse the five recommendations regarding refugees which appear in the final report of the dialogue;

2) that the WCC and its member churches reaffirm clearly our Christian practice of serving all refugees regardless of their religion, and continue to study and analyze the causes of refugee situations which are often complex and of a socio-political, religious and racial character;

3) that the WCC encourage cooperation wherever possible at the national and local level between Christians, Muslims and all other institutions in meeting the immediate and long-range needs of refugees, working within the context of the policies of the receiving countries;

4) that the WCC express its readiness to consult with appropriate Islamic organizations to consider all aspects of the refugee problem, with the understanding that such consultation be carried out within the context of international agencies dealing with refugee issues, such as UNHCR, and on the part of the WCC within the existing structures of church work for refugees;

5) that, in view of the fact that many of today's refugees in the world are of Muslim religion, the WCC express its readiness to discuss the deeper complex issues which have led to this alarming phenomenon and to undertake whatever action or initiative may be appropriate;

6) that the WCC reaffirm that the ultimate goal of work among refugees is repatriation to the country from which they have fled, and failing this refer to WCC resolutions dealing with other possible solutions.

V. Regarding minorities, we recommend:

1) that the WCC affirm the recommendations on minorities, while recognizing that the whole concept of majority and minority needs further study;

2) that the question of minorities be further discussed in the framework of human rights, recognizing that basic human rights are of three categories: individual rights, rights of smaller communities (including those cases where identity is based on religion), and the rights of the larger society; in emphasizing the rights of the smaller communities, it is recognized that this may conflict with individual rights, and might in turn force groups and individuals into ghetto-like situations; thus, a balance has to be sought between individual rights, the rights of the smaller communities, and the unity and ethos of the wider society;

3) that in the continuing dialogue on minorities, the tensions mentioned in the preamble of the report on minorities should be expected to include:
   a) tensions between different historical perspectives and theological perceptions;
   b) tensions between ideals and realities;
   c) tensions between the different realities.

VI. Comments for future implementation of Christian-Muslim cooperation:

1. In order to give support to the DFI and the WCC at large in facing the ongoing dialogue with the Muslim partners, it is essential that a network of Christian consultants be established which can be drawn upon for information and expertise.

2. It is important that Christians identify and make known their preoccupations in pursuit of dialogue. It is urged that studies continue with regard to the issues of legitimate diakonia and evangelism, and the misuse of diakonia and evangelism as a form of proselytism.

3. Several points in the final report of the dialogue should be read against the background that Christians should be sensitive to the desire of many Muslims to relate common projects to a mutual understanding of the whole philosophy of development.

4. It would be important to make an effort to bring the findings of the WCC in the field of development, and the relation between science and revelation, reason and faith into relation with the dialogue with our Muslim partners and where possible to bring their ideas into our own focus, as well as our ideas into their focus.

5. With regard to recommendation A.7 of the final report of the dialogue we are convinced that the problems mentioned there are of utmost importance to both parties. We support the idea of constituting bilateral working groups on the topics mentioned. We would urge very strongly that DFI cooperate with other WCC sub-units in promoting as soon as possible a thorough study from the Christian side on these problems. We are deeply convinced of the necessity of preparing Christians for dialogue with Muslim partners, and we call on church authorities, national and regional councils of churches, Christian study centres, and the WCC to promote such preparation.

Participants

Christians

Delegates

Mr Kodwo Ankrah
Uganda/Ghana

Dr John Berthrong
Canada

Rev. Roby Bois
France

Fr Angel Calvo
Philippines

Dr James Cogswell
USA

Mrs Mary Fadel
Egypt

Sr Fatima Prakasam
India

Mrs Margaret Greene
Sierra Leone

Bishop Grégoire Haddad
Lebanon

Dr Ihromi
Indonesia

Rev. Stanley Jeyaraj
Sri Lanka

Fr Michel Lelong
France

Dr U.N. Malakar
Bangladesh

Bishop Alexander Malik
Pakistan

Fr Tom Michel
Vatican

Dr D.C. Mulder
Netherlands

Dr Jürgen Micksch
Federal Republic of Germany

Fr Augustin Nikitin
USSR

Mr Cees van der Poort
Netherlands

Rev. Ian Roach
The Gambia

Rev. E. Ramtu
Kenya

Mr Elie Romba
Chad

Dr Olaf Schumann
Federal Republic of Germany

Dr T.B. Simatupang
Indonesia

Rev. F. Suleiman Greis
Sudan

Rev. Tan Chi Kiong
Malaysia

Bishop Henri Teissier
Algeria

Fr A. Tilahun
Ethiopia

Rev. R. Ward
Kenya/Canada

OKR Klaus Wilkens
Federal Republic of Germany

Observers

Sus Abharatna
Mrs T.B. Irving
Mrs K. Wilkens

Secretariat

Dr John B. Taylor
Mr Jean Fischer
Mr Ghassan Rubeiz
Mrs Jean Spechter

Interpreters

Mrs Nicole Fischer
Mr Heinz Birchmeier

Muslims

Delegates

H.E. Dr Marouf Al Daoualibi
President, World Muslim Congress

Hon. M. Haniffa Mohamed
Minister, Sri Lanka

Sayed Haider Al-Husseini
Deputy S.G.

Dr Ahmed D. Alonto
Philippines

Mr Abdus Salam Morita
Japan

Mr Yunus Saleen
India

Sheikh Hashim Al-Mojaddedi
Afghanistan

Sheikh Eisa Bin Nasser
United Arab Emirates

Mr B. Tarzi Kamel
Tunisia

Dr Aboubakr el Kadiri
Morocco

Hon. Abubakar Mayanja
Uganda

Mr Haji Mohamed Khan
Singapore

Dr Rifat M. Yucelten
Motamar-Cyprus

Dr A.H. Tabibi
Motamar-UN-Switzerland

Dr Viqar Hamdani
Motamar-UN-USA

Mr I. Ahmed Imtiazi
Pakistan

Mr Ahmed Kemal
Organization of the Islamic
Conference

Mr M.H. Faruqi
Impact Institute, UK

Dr A. Fuad Shaheen
Canada

Dr T.B. Irving
USA

Dr Kalil Abdel Alim
Indonesia

Prof. Ahmad Saddali
Indonesia

Mr Ahmad Sahirul Alim
Indonesia

Mr Fadlullah Wilmot
Regional Islamic Da'wah Court
of Southeast Asia and the Pacific

Mr A. Sinaceur
Unesco

Prof. Abdul Majid Mackeen
Sri Lanka

Dr Badria al Aawadhi
Motamar

Dr Roqaiya V. Mangalett
Philippines

Dr Mohamed I. Momoniat
South Africa

Dr Y. Najmuddin
India

Prof. Khurshid Ahmed
Islamic Foundation, UK

Mr M.A. Abdullah
Federal Republic of Germany

Mr Ahmed Von Denffer
Islamic Foundation, UK

Observers

Hon. M.L.M. Aboossally
Sri Lanka

Mr Moulana Jamal Mian
Motamar

Mr Khalid Ikramullah Khan
World Muslim Congress

Mr R.J.M. Ariff
Sri Lanka

Mr Djailan
Indonesia

Dr Hisham Ahmed
Canada

Mr Ustad M. Alouini
Belgium

Secretariat

Mr S.I. Jafferjee
Dr Hasonnah
Mr M.I. Kaleel

Regional Colloquia
1983-1989

III. 1
Religion and Responsibility

3 March 1986

The francophone West African Christian-Muslim colloquium organized by the WCC (Porto Novo, Benin, 3-7 March 1986) began its first session with common prayer and a common exhortation: put our works in the care of God, asking that this meeting might contribute to understanding between believers.

During the presentations, each participant expressed concern that we should dialogue to get better acquainted with each other and to learn to respect each other better, and eventually to commit ourselves to a common effort.

The participants came from a range of backgrounds: theologians, lay academics, journalists, teachers, Christians and Muslims of varying tendencies: everyday, ordinary people.

We approved the programme as presented.

4 March: Religion and state — Abdul Karim Cisse, Dominique Sarr
5 March: Religion and education — Grace Dossou, Saliou Kandji
6 March: Religion and family — Seydou Diallo, Elie Miloungou
7 March: Closing session

Presidents: Rev. Harry Henry, President of the Protestant Methodist Church of Benin. Mr Muhammad Saleh Hamid, Interfaith Relations Officer for the World Muslim League.

● This text has been translated from the French by the editor.

Secretaries: El Hadj Harouna Sana, member of the Muslim Community Association of Ouagadougou, Burkina Faso. Eugénie R. Aw, communications officer, All Africa Conference of Churches.

4 March 1986 — Topic I: Religion and state

The first paper was read by Mr Dominique Sarr, professor in the Faculty of Law at the University of Dakar, Senegal.

A preliminary concern relates to the gap between formal talk about the state and the realities of Africa. The state is artificial, imposed, and it would be helpful to adapt it to our traditional culture in order to make its institutions more effective. In Africa, state formation is conditioned by the religious milieu, and it is impossible to ignore the sacred dimension of power. So we must closely examine the concept of secularity: does it conform to our realities or not? Is it a vehicle of all sorts of modernity (critical thought, toleration, freedom...)?

Is secularity necessary and how can it be situated in the African context? Here are some definitions.

a) It is characteristic of everything that is confessional without being clerical.

b) It can go further and be non-confessional. It is reason as distinct from faith, temporal in relation to the spiritual. This idea finds expression in the elaboration of sovereign political and juridical institutions.

In the African sense, it is a positive non-confessionalism, seeking to guarantee and respect plurality in the search for national unity.

How can this secularity be protected?

— by establishing a national pact with a formula for living together, for encounter or dialogue which would allow our cultural and historical genius to express itself on behalf of the popular will to build an organic unity in a plural context;

— by guaranteeing freedom of religion: different laws must provide for the non-confessionality of the state and encourage the development of each religious community: this is just a question of helping Africa find afresh its traditions of mutual respect.

* * *

The second lecture, by Dr Abdoul Karim Cissé of Ivory Coast, described the Islamic state.

From the Islamic point of view, only God, who is free from any influence, can judge according to the truth. There is no judgment outside the judgment of God. As a result, sovereignty belongs to God, who delegates it. So there is no clergy, no monopoly in the interpretation of sacred texts, and laws are not immutable; any legislation can be changed that is not codified in the Qur'an and the Sunnah.

Rulers must have three qualities: knowledge, fear of God and a sense of justice. They are mandataries in the service of the people. Their duties and responsibilities materialize in institutions which allow the law of God to be enforced, e.g. in the protection of Islamic territory and the establishment of justice, development and prosperity for all.

Citizenship is determined not by a territorial frontier but by the Islamic faith, which requires a declaration of faith, respect for the pillars of Islam and the shari'ah (law codifying life-style, effort in the way of virtue, love of neighbour...). Non-Muslims may also be citizens, as long as they respect the state and its laws and pay a special tax to help the state protect them.

If the leader fills the conditions noted above, the community is obliged to obey, support and advise him.

The legitimacy of the Islamic state

Power is based on consultation. There is no basis of privilege other than religious behaviour and intellectual competence. All men are slaves of God and each may attain knowledge by studying the Qur'an, the Sunnah, jurisprudence and the consensus of Islamic scholars.

In terms of foreign policy, the Islamic state works through peaceful means. It defends justice, the weak and Islamic minorities, but struggles against anyone who attacks it.

Finally, the lecturer noted that the Islamic state is today an ideal, even though there once was a model Islamic state (in Medina in the time of the Prophet).

Discussion

1. We felt a need to define the state about which we were talking, in order to situate its power over the believers.

— Which state is under scrutiny? It is the Western notion of the state, with its political institutions.

— What is its relationship to religion? It should guarantee a plural society.

— Religions tend to influence the state. They have the same focus: individual, law, citizen. How can believers contribute positively to the state's wellbeing?

2. We reviewed the historical and political contexts:

Islam: knew (at Medina, in the Prophet's day) a state which perfectly formed the link between the temporal and the spiritual. This state provided for all types of person; the Qur'an is a comprehensive blueprint for society.

Christianity: offers a message of love, justice and a separation of powers which does not excuse us from involvement (render to Caesar the things that are Caesar's).

In religious conflicts (crusades, jihads...) each side has sought to appropriate God. There comes a moment in history when the spiritual abandons the temporal. Now, we have similar codes and a common notion that power comes from God. This ought to lead us to universal community based on such spiritual values as love and justice.

3. Temporal and spiritual: This is the challenge before us as Africans. We have inherited a type of state and also religions which we have not made the effort to assimilate fully into our being, our cultural and historical identity.

a) We should reappropriate freedom of conscience and religion as a characteristic of the black African people, and so pass from plurality to pluralism, allowing all to live together in mutual respect.

b) Religion ought to have an interest in the question of the state. Our convictions as believers is a force for changing attitudes to people and society in the direction of a genuine humanization. This is especially so when the state becomes estranged from the community.

4. Diversity is an asset: This is the whole point of our meeting. The choice of topics is designed primarily to help us move forward together and to get to know each other, so we can grow in respect towards love and common endeavour in the service of society and humanity. The sincere believer must always have a receptive and conscientious attitude: by changing ourselves we bear witness to the truth.

The group associated itself with this phrase from the Bible: "You shall know the truth and the truth shall make you free." But this requires a commitment from the believers. God really does not change human situations until we change our own behaviour (Qur'an 13:7).

5 March 1986 — Topic II: Religion and education

The first lecture was actually about teaching, with some reference to education. Mrs Grace Dossou, the speaker, is director of inspections and methods in the Beninese Ministry of Middle and Higher Education.

Everyone is aware of the importance of education. Already in biblical times, we have a saying attributed to King Solomon (Book of Proverbs): "The teaching of the wise is a source of life for avoiding the clutches of death." And: "Instruct a child in the way it should go, and when grown the person will not go astray."

What relations are there between religions, particularly Christianity and Islam, and teaching? These two religions expound belief in one God, a life hereafter, resurrection and the last judgment. They set rules in an organized, explicit way for Muslims, governing the life of a believer who has submitted to God; more generally for Christians, through love of neighbour.

How can these religions be placed in terms of teaching which seeks to pass on different types of awareness (scientific, technical, social...), through the means of various structures or simply by living experience? Teaching aims at training the whole person and making certain skills available to society, as well as helping the individual to assume responsibility for oneself. The acquisition of awareness and practical knowledge thus encounters a message addressed to believers: the call to bring the good news, the command to give to others and to recognize the seal of the Creator as one discovers the universe.

Teaching and religion are not mutually exclusive. History confirms this, for schools, colleges, institutions of higher learning were first of all the concerns of the religious before the principle of secularity became common. Similarly, Islam depends on the Qur'anic schools. Parallel to secular instruction, there is religious instruction.

The fact that certain states have queried the responsibility of religious leaders for education poses a question: what role do Islam and Christianity have today? They have a primordial responsibility in education and conscientization. Are they not abdicating their role of forming competent personalities "whose light shall indeed shine before the world"? What concrete initiatives are possible in the moral education of children that will help them respond to the needs imposed by society?

The ensuing discussion concentrated on education.

1. Some perceptions

— A person is not a random sower. The child is led by the mother, who is the first educator.
— In the hands of an educator, a child is like a creeping plant, creeping only in the directions set out by the educator.

— Education once received remains indelibly printed on the personality. (From these premises there develops the perspective which would orient education in a particular direction.)

2. Some problems
— Every African is living an ambiguous adventure which has triggered a crisis of values, of religion and, consequently, of school and society.
— Education may be defined as the socialization of the individual from childhood onwards. It has three components: institutions of various forms; a process leading to awareness, knowledge and especially a capacity to be; a finished subject which acts and influences the surroundings.
What socialization do we want? This is the crux of the whole problem. Here are some elements:
— Teaching should be part of education. Nowadays it is not well integrated with the life and specific conditions of our societies. Education is therefore in crisis because it is not dealing with the development of our children, given that it imitates foreign models.
— Children and young people tend to reject religious values as a moral foundation for all teaching. We must allocate responsibilities (environment, over-aggressive advertizing, family dislocations, inadequate teachers...).
— Religious instruction does not answer the real needs; it addresses real life less and less: it does not keep pace with the pupil at each stage of growth. Religious instruction remains at a primary level, unadapted to scientific discoveries and general intellectual development.

3. Some answers
We have only looked at education and teaching from the perspectives of yesterday (colonial school) and today (independence). We must recapture the initiatory character of traditional education and revive our acculturation as the basis of creativity and access to science and technology following our own patterns. We must go to the root of our social problems in search of effective solutions (delinquency, prostitution, drugs...).
We can build a plural society with unity of faith in its fundamental elements. We should teach Christian children about Islam and Muslim children about Christianity.

* * *

The second lecture was given by Mr Saliou Kandji, a retired journalist and former ambassador, from Senegal.

It is important to consider the place of the religions in the school curricula by linking these religions to their evolution in the Black African world.

Black African theology was based on a pluralist monotheism rooted in belief in the existence of a first principle (the Creator), specific pure spirits who sustain order and harmony, disembodied spirits who have been sanctified or reproved, and the spirits of the living-dead in process of sanctification or reproduction. Humans may enter into contact with these three last groups. Evil or disorder, good or order do not exist in themselves, but in function of harmony and community.

So can the fact of being Muslim or Christian allow one to proclaim one's faith without forsaking our cultural and linguistic specificity?...

Let us look at Islam: its principles derive from belief, knowledge and action.

— Belief evokes the representation which each of us makes of God. The Qur'an cites the appearance of prophets as a necessity for every human community. Each prophet is born into a culture and transmits a message in a language; this is the message of the Omnipresent heard as part of the absolute truth.

— Knowledge: the message underpinning the faith is intrinsically cultural and appeals to people's experience.

— Action: interpersonal relations, in all their civil, penal and financial codes, are adaptable because they often overlay an order which existed before the introduction of Islam.

Africa has known three periods of religious instruction:

— Peaceful internal multilingualism: pre-Islamic religious teaching articulated in national languages with the object of producing an integrated social being (with social and communal attributes). The spirit informs and commands the material.

— Peaceful internal bilingualism (10th-19th century). This appeared with the Islamization of the African masses. Arabic is the vector of Islamic consciousness, so a minority instructed their coreligionaries in their own languages, at all levels. The pupils heard the Arabic text explained and commented on in their own languages; this facilitated the elaboration of local grammars and the enrichment of vernacular vocabularies (e.g. scientific concepts). Islam thus became an integral part of black African values.

— Exclusive unilingualism: this is the fruit of the Western school. It becomes impossible to pass on knowledge in the local language, so citizens are estranged from their own surroundings.

Today we ask: what religious dimension, what programmes can we introduce into our teaching to focus on one immanent, transcendent God?

The real challenge is to free ourselves from outside domination, recover our virtues of inculcating responsibility and initiative through a spiritual, scientific and cultural revolution.

Discussion

Most of the questions raised sought clarification or elaboration. It was stressed that religious history, the authentic God-person relationship, did not begin with Islam and Christianity.

— Initiation should follow the black African pattern of a constant assimilation of information "from the cradle to the grave". Priests were a source of knowledge.
— Can we live according to Qur'an by building on Black African values? Without in any way diminishing the Qur'anic revelation, we must not forget that the Qur'an is an "ahistorical" book. In fact, what we must do is renew the understanding of the message.
— Fatalism or predestination are less important than the believer's responsibility.
— The first talk noted the crisis in education; the second talk complemented it by immersing us in a re-examination of foreign influences. We must rediscover our own imagination.
— Through consensus, we should work together to trace adequate channels of information.

6 March 1986 — Topic III: Religion and family

The first address was by Seydou Diallo, retired labour inspector from Bamako, Mali.

These three days of dialogue have taken us to the very depths of human history, especially of those people who refuse to close themselves into small spaces but prefer to live openly in our own era. The family is the grouping which unites individuals by ties of blood, of solidarity. It is the basic cell of society.

Religion is a pillar of society, a source of inspiration which guides us in our daily life. Without faith, there is no real family which is a physical unit that also embraces the human virtues of love and faithfulness. When the family dissolves, it is the whole society which suffers. Respect for the family is therefore a duty for the believers. In understanding its role, we encounter the phenomenon of mixed marriages. What is the Muslim attitude to this?

Often people take positions in order to maintain a balance, to provide for the education of children or simply out of ignorance, and so obstruct communication and harm the relations they wished to foster. A colloquium ought to facilitate the fraternal discussion of these questions in the common quest for a reconciliation.

* * *

The second presentation was made by Rev. Elie Miloungou of the Burkina Faso Apostolic Mission. *The Goal:* a search for fraternity.

What is religion? It is an ultimate preoccupation which makes all other concerns provisional. Black Africans filled every aspect of their life with this religion in the vision of a spiritualized world that included everything visible and, especially, invisible. Islam and Christianity appeared later.

As for marriage, this is the voluntary, solemn union of a man and a woman in order to establish a family. Islam forbids marriage with idolators but allows Muslim men to marry Christian or Jewish women. This is because Christians and Jews, as People of the Book, believe in the one God and understand the difference between good and evil.

Within a given family there may be resistance to a mixed marriage. This is generally based on a subjective appreciation or on observed behaviour that is inconsistent with the texts. Some Christians fear that their daughters will be mistreated (forced conversion, polygamy...). In spite of these obstacles, such marriages occur, for the young are often reckless in the face of opposition. Why do Christians have this attitude when people of the two faiths are often members of the same family? Neither Christians nor Muslims want to be importuned by the others on questions of theology or doctrine, because disputes of this order do not help the cohabitation made necessary by the social environment in Africa. Mixed marriages may be considered as a venue for dialogue and sharing where people live their faith in God without constraint.

DISCUSSION

1. The family in the texts and in real life

a) *Mixed marriages:* Muslims may not marry idolators who raise other divinities to equality with the one true God. A Muslim woman may not marry a non-Muslim because this would put her under the authority of a man whose basic beliefs diverged from hers.

Someone asked whether these restrictions were absolute or designed to safeguard the family from a disturbance due to religious causes. Can we distinguish the letter from the spirit of the verses in question? The message has an identical content (God is One; do good), and the family is a cultural entity in relationship with the surrounding community. It would, thought some, be helpful to consider these verses in their dynamic evolution. Christianity permits mixed marriages and each partner is free to practise his/her religion. The non-Christian spouse is sanctified by the Christian partner.

b) *Polygamy and divorce:* Polygamy was a pre-Islamic practice which Islam has codified and limited with the object of guaranteeing equal treatment for the wives. Besides, a woman can refuse a polygamous relationship. It is important to remember that divorce sometimes happens, in spite of strong opposition in some monotheistic settings. According to both Christianity and Islam, divorce is undesirable. The Qur'anic text condones divorce when the two parties concur.

Christianity officially forbids polygamy, even though some men are clandestine polygamists. Divorce is discouraged because it is bad to separate what God has joined. All accommodations at this level are simply compensations for human weakness.

c) *The role of women:* In the practice of the two religions, certain prescriptions are used to confirm privileges. Is it not an insult to God's creation if we keep one of God's creatures in weakness, ignorance which prevents her from practising her faith, witnessing to her belief and defending her ideas in an adult, responsible manner? How can we start a dialogue that will help woman to assume her full role as an educator on an equal footing with her partner?

Woman must be freed so she can truly make the choices which the texts invite her to make. Here, too, we must remember that each community organizes the type of family which it desires, and we must be constantly aware of the changing times in order for our message to remain valid.

2. The family and its preoccupations

a) *Family and education:* (1) Mixed marriages raise questions about the education of children. It is important to sustain a dialogue in the unity of faith. (2) Research is needed on the evolution of families in our societies. The family is an institution in danger because of economic conditions, the influence of the media and the questioning of value systems by the young.

The uncertainty of the future causes anxieties. What policies do the religions propose regarding the family?

b) *Family and knowledge:* Science has brought certain prescriptions into question, e.g. about procreation, which classically was to be realized within the family context. Religious leaders need to reflect on such subjects as artificial insemination and birth control.

3. Some tentative solutions

a) *Some observations:* There is a gap between the texts and real life. It is necessary to understand the actual situation in order to respond as persons of faith with a pastoral attitude. At the same time, the message must be lived without hypocrisy, in a dynamic of sharing and sincerity.

What is harmful is the way we live. We are brought into question by our life-style and we must rid it of all its vices. Each person should fairly interpret the other's message. We will come together on the basic elements and differ on details. It is important to insist on what unites us and respect our differences.

b) *What to do?* For a genuine dialogue we must give priority to the Love which will help us to meet each other. It is therefore essential to make each member of our communities, each believer, aware of our concerns in order to change social attitudes. In this respect, we shall have to act on what we have worked out together during this colloquium. We must share the wealth of what we have learned in order to banish false impressions and find our African roots.

A provisional conclusion

We reached a sincere and mutual understanding on the following points:

1. Both the Islamic and the Christian messages can be passed on through instruction with a view to educating God's creatures in a manner which supports the spiritual development of these creatures.

2. We must question anew those alienating foreign influences which inhibit the flowering of the personality, whether they are of Islamic or Christian provenance. We must reaffirm our common African values.

3. Africans firmly believe that a person is an indivisible entity; there is no distinction between spiritual and social aspects. A return to our origins is the essential element which will help us put down new roots in our adopted faith, be it Christianity or Islam.

Participants

Muslims

M. Liamidi Younoussa Adegbidin
BP 139, Porto Novo, Benin

M. Hamza Alassane
BP 6, Djougou, Benin

M.A. Gafar Badre-Deen
BP 399, Porto Novo, Benin

Dr Abdul Karim Cisse
08 BP 2098
Abidjan 08, Ivory Coast

El Hadj Moussedik Damala
BP 1178, Porto Novo, Benin

M. Kamarou Daouda
BP 378, Porto Novo, Benin

M. Seydou Diallo
BP 559, Bamako, Mali

El Hadj Machioudi Dissou
BP 515, Porto Novo, Benin

El Hadj Muhammad Saleh Hamid
World Muslim League
2 bis ch. Auguste-Vilbert
1218 Gd. Saconnex, Switzerland

M. Saliou Kandji
Cité de la Patte d'Oie
Builders Villa A21
Dakar, Senegal

M. Rafiji Latoundji
BP 1506, Porto Novo, Benin

Dr Saliou Latoundji
BP 63, Mfou, Cameroon

Dr Mamadou Ndiaye
University of Dakar
BP 2639, Dakar, Senegal

El Hadj Harouna Sana
BP 7034 Ouagadougou, Burkina Faso

M.A. Badre Tadj-Deen
BP 1596, Porto Novo, Benin

El Hadj Amamou Taminou
Director, Centre d'études islamiques
BP 6, Djougou, Benin

Christians

M. Moïse Aderomou
BP 491, Porto Novo, Benin

M. Daniel Akinocho
BP 44, Porto Novo, Benin

Pasteur Samson Assani
Eglise apostolique
BP 03-0818
Cotonou, Benin

Pasteur Esaie Ategbo
BP 713, Porto Novo, Benin

Abbé Siméon Atsain
04 BP 119
Abidjan 04, Ivory Coast

Mme Eugénie Aw
AACC
P.O. Box 14205
Nairobi, Kenya

M. Samuel Boton
BP 32, Porto Novo, Benin

Mme Monique Brasse
Eglise protestante du Sénégal
BP 847, Dakar, Senegal

Dr Stuart E. Brown
Christian-Muslim Relations
World Council of Churches
BP 66
1211 Geneva 20, Switzerland

R.P. Jean-Baptiste Camara
BP 105, Conakry, Guinea

Bernard C. Catraye
BP 68, Ouidah, Benin

Pasteur Esai K. Daoudou
BP 37, Djougou, Benin

Mme Grace Dossou
BP 1069, Porto Novo, Benin

Mgr Jean-Rigal Elisee
Box 51, Banjul, Gambia

Pasteur Harry Y. Henry
President, Eglise méthodiste du Bénin
BP 34, Cotonou, Benin

Pasteur Elie Miloungou
Mission apostolique du Burkina Faso
BP 176, Porto Novo, Benin

Pasteur Jacques Ndensi
Equipe du Sahel du COE
BP 1006, Ougadougou, Burkina Faso

Abbé Georges Oloude
BP 62, Pobè, Benin

Dr Paluku-Rubinga
Dean, Faculty of Evangelical
Theology
BP 988
Bangui, Central African Republic

Mr Paul Sai
Eglise méthodiste du Bénin
BP 485, Porto Novo, Benin

Dr Dominique Sarr
Faculty of Law
University of Dakar
Dakar, Senegal

M. Emile Sodjinou
BP 137, Porto Novo, Benin

III. 2
Advancing Together into the Next Century

6 December 1986

Chairmen:
Dr Inamullah Khan, general secretary, World Muslim Congress, Karachi
Rev. Dr Soritua A. Nababan, president, Communion of Churches in Indonesia, Jakarta

Rapporteurs:
Rev. Akuila Yabaki, secretary for communication, Fiji Methodist Church, Suva. El-Hajj Fadlullah Wilmot, director for information, Regional Islamic Da'wah Council for Southeast Asia and the Pacific, Kuala Lumpur

The meeting approved the programme as presented:

7 December 1986: Religion and the state
8 December 1986: Religion and economics
9 December 1986: Religion and the family
10 December 1986: Closing session

The colloquium was officially opened by H.A. Ludjito, director of religious research and deveopment in the Indonesian Ministry of Religious Affairs, and a brief message from Governor Mantra of Bali was heard. Dr T.B. Simatupang (a retired general) then read an introductory paper on dialogue in Indonesia, and Dr Amin Rais (delegate of Indonesian Muslim Congress) spoke on Indonesian Islam.

The ensuing discussion underlined both the importance of shari'ah for Muslims and the Christians' concern that all laws should be fairly and consistently applied. There was a general dislike of unfair proselytism and a shared feeling of responsibility to God and accountability for actions in this world.

7 December 1986 — Theme I: Religion and the state

The two speakers were: Prof. Dr Asghar Ali Engineer, director of the Institute of Islamic Studies, Bombay, and Rev. Dr Hilario M. Gomez, Jr, professor of Asian religion, Union Theological Seminary, Manila.

There was considerable discussion on the issue of the Islamic state. Many Muslim participants were of the opinion that the Muslims in a country where they formed the absolute majority should endeavour to introduce shari'ah as the basic law of the land. However, the Muslims were eager to dissociate the idea of an Islamic state from the imposition of certain punishments or oppression, and several Muslims felt strongly that states with Muslim majorities should not uncritically impose the shari'ah set forth by a small group of 'ulama' but establish a consensus consistent with contemporary circumstances; certain aspects of *fiqh* should be re-examined in the light of contemporary realities. All the Muslims agreed that the basic concept of the Islamic state was the establishment of justice, and socio-economic justice was emphasized. Most of the Muslims would like Muslim minorities to have recourse to the provisions of Muslim personal law.

Some of the Christian participants raised questions about the rights of non-Muslims and the rights of women in an Islamic state. The question of separate electorates for non-Muslims in Pakistan was noted. The participants were of the opinion that if non-Muslims did not want separate electorates, they should not be forced to have them. It was explained that the Islamic concept did not involve a single pattern for all citizens but that the Islamic state was a federation of different communities united but having their separate cultures, languages, institutions and personal law. The ideal Islamic state was just and provided a two-way channel of communication with the leadership consulting the people and the people constructively criticizing the leaders.

Regarding the question of conversion and the overtones of words such as "proselytize" and "evangelize", Muslims felt that the Chambésy declaration should be implemented. They said they felt very uneasy about mission activities aimed at Muslims and uneasy about Muslims being converted.

A number of the Christian participants expressed their discomfort with the concept of an Islamic state which enforced the shari'ah. They would prefer to see the state as either neutral regarding religion or supporting all religions.

Muslims said that they were open to criticism about their implementation of human rights and socio-economic justice. The need for the location of an Islamic socio-economic environment was emphasized.

The Christian churches had supported the political rights of Muslims in the Philippines and their claim to autonomy, as well as to the establishment of shari'ah courts for Muslim personal law. The participants emphasized that religious people must find ways of dealing with such problems, and of contributing towards the design of general development programmes.

Apart from the different attitudes towards the state, where Muslims and Christians agreed to disagree, there was a great deal of agreement on many issues regarding the relationship of Muslims and Christians, as people of religion, to the state. Both Muslims and Christians emphasized the fundamental concept of justice for all. The need for the state to deal with the problem of poverty and the unequal distribution of wealth was stressed. Muslims and Christians, it was agreed, should work together to bring justice to all the people.

The participants were agreed that there was a need to democratize totalitarian regimes and find ways of dealing with the erosion of human rights, the torture and imprisonment of political dissidents and the suffocating role of bureaucracies. People of religion should work for the oppressed.

There was a danger that the political elites in developing countries might use the slogans of national unity, national security and national development to oppress the people in order to maintain themselves in power. There was, it was felt, a need to develop a means of making a critique of the governments.

Another matter discussed was the power of the people. It was felt that Muslims and Christians should work together to give power to the people. Structures and systems should be developed in order to ensure that the masses as well as the elites share in political decisions.

The Asia-Pacific countries have moved from a post-colonial to a neo-colonial situation, which means that they still depend on others for their science and technology, food, information, and culture. Muslims and Christians should work together to define programmes to overcome such dependency. The enormous debt of third-world countries has made the state dependent on others, and people of religion should help find ways to ensure that their states overcome the major problems of our time, such as environmental pollution, the depletion of national resources and the need to increase agricultural production.

Very often both Muslim and Christian leaders and their institutions have taken the side of the oppressors against the masses. Sincere believers should work to restore the proper solidarity between people of faith and the poor.

None of the Christian participants saw any need to establish a Christian state ruled by the church. All were of the opinion that the relationship between Christians, the church and the state should be one of critical participation, where the church critically participates in the socio-political processes so as to bring about non-violent changes in society. The Christians felt that church and state should generally be free from each other as they operate on different although interacting levels. The example of the role of the churches in achieving the people's peaceful revolution in the Philippines was cited.

8 December 1986 — Theme II: Religion and economics

The speakers were Dr David Chellappa, bursar of the Tamilnadu Theological Seminary, Madurai, and Dr Mushirul Haq, professor of Islamic studies, Jamia Millia Islamia, New Delhi.

Christians and Muslims agreed that leaders and institutions of their faiths had often sided with the oppressors and had not fulfilled their duties to the oppressed. Both religions have a definite stand on economic issues, and participants agreed that economics was not value-neutral and that people of religion should seek to inform their fellows that religion actually has a stand vis-à-vis economic issues.

A number of the Christian participants seemed to feel that some of the answers to the economic problems could be found in socialist theories and they emphasized the Christian concern for the poor. While Muslims held that Islam also laid great emphasis on equality and the prevention of poverty, several felt that the solution could not be found in socialism, for many thought that the Qur'an and Sunnah had laid the framework for a just economic system. Some Muslim participants rejected both the capitalist and socialist models and appealed to Muslim religious and economic experts to elucidate a distinctively Islamic approach to economics; for them, Muslim leaders should have confidence in Islam and not believe half in Islam and half in something else. Other Muslims, however, suggested that the framework of Qur'an and Sunnah did not foreclose any options and urged careful consideration of all ideas which could possibly enhance socio-economic justice; even socialism deserved examination, according to these participants.

Muslims and Christians agreed that structural changes were necessary in virtually all economies. The participants refused to accept an unjust objective reality as an invariable, and they shared the opinion that religious people should do their best to change an unjust status quo.

It was pointed out that many religious leaders were ignorant of the different models of development being followed by their governments, and did not understand the exploitative nature of existing systems. Many participants evoked the need for alternative models.

Many economic systems are controlled by the political elite. Many religious people do not understand the power structure and an exploitative economic system is often clothed in some high-sounding approach.

All participants expressed concern at the potential disaster, which could ruin mankind if present policies were continued:

1) increasing poverty;
2) increasing unemployment among both educated and uneducated;
3) accumulation of wealth in fewer and fewer hands;
4) increase in urbanization;
5) increasing homelessness and squatter settlements;
6) the breakdown of urban transport;
7) increasing centralization and political despotism; and
8) increases in crime and juvenile delinquency.

It was suggested that basic questions should be asked about the type of technology to be used, and the forms of development required. Education systems, it was felt, should encourage cultural enlightenment and social responsibility.

Muslims and Christians agreed that planning was necessary to break Asia's excessive dependency on others. Men of religion should, with experts in the various fields, work out alternative forms of development.

Muslims and Christians were concerned that there was a need among their respective faith communities to develop moral attitudes towards wealth and economic development, but participants agreed that moral sermonizing alone could achieve nothing. There was a need to examine present structures with a view to changing the unjust and exploitative elements into something fairer.

It was felt that religious leaders needed to be better informed about the role of transnational corporations as well as the increasing concentration of economic power in fewer and fewer hands, wherever this is happening.

The Muslims pointed out that monopolies were forbidden under Islamic shari'ah.

The consumer society, which considers the consumption of goods and services as the ultimate goal of economic activity, was discussed. The Muslims emphasized that extravagance was forbidden in Islam. The destructive effects of modern advertising were discussed and people of each religion felt that some control over advertising was needed.

As an effective means of dealing with poverty, Muslims said that it was the duty of the state to ensure the effective collection and distribution of zakat. In the opinion of several Christians almsgiving did not offer an adequate answer to poverty, which could be properly treated only through the promotion of economic justice. Existing unjust economic systems can be changed only by a change in power structures.

Muslims and Christians agreed that as people of religion they had a duty to educate their faith communities about the amount of money allocated in their countries to defence or munitions. They should bring pressure to bear on all governments to limit spending on armaments and defence, which was completely unproductive. The potential crisis facing the third world if its raw materials become obsolete was seen as an issue of concern to people of faith.

In search for economic and social justice, the Christian concept of stewardship and the Muslim concept of man's servitude to God and his role as vice-gerent were most relevant. People of religion should develop an awareness of the future and the perception to relate the teachings of their faiths to current problems and meet the challenges of the future with practical solutions.

9 December 1986 — Theme III: Religion and the family

Papers were read by Prof. Dr Carmen A. Abubakar, dean of the Institute of Islamic Studies, University of the Philippines, Manila, and Rev. Martin Adhikary, a member of the WCC Dialogue Commission, from Gopalganj, Bangladesh.

Christian and Muslim participants alike expressed concern over the disintegration of the family in many parts of the world, including their own countries. As members of families, many people are increasingly confused about the sacred meaning of life in relation to their fellow humans in society at large and in local neighbourhoods. The family as an institution could best be understood in the context of a world-view related to and shaped by religion. The family was seen as the basic unit of moral education for future generations.

Efforts should be redoubled to adapt the methods of religious instruction to the changing conditions of modern life. Schools and governments should also give freedom to girls to wear the clothing that their parents consider acceptable within the precepts of their religion.

The changing role of women was discussed as more and more mothers participate in the work force. It was felt that the care of children is a joint responsibility of husband and wife. However, since in early childhood mothers need to be close to children, facilities for child care should be provided. Medical and psychological benefits of breast-feeding were emphasized. Motherhood should not be a pretext for denying women a more equal role in society.

All participants agreed on the need to care for parents in their old age. The problems of child abuse and the situation of the children of divorced parents were discussed. The sexual revolution has broken down family traditions and religious moral standards but the family seemed unprepared to deal with this challenge. Guidance is needed to prepare parents and children for the future.

Participants felt people of religion had a duty to bring pressure on those in authority to look carefully at the philosophy of life and dubious transnational values provided in the mass media, particularly in television, which has now become in too many places a medium to propagate a violent, amoral, immoral, irreligious and sensate culture.

When people remain in conditions of poverty lacking the basic essentials of life, living in deplorable slum conditions, the establishment of a healthy family life is impossible. The poor do not always accept the moral and ethical values of religion. Christians and Muslims must be seen to be working to transform such unjust economic conditions.

Children these days are not likely to listen to sermons, homilies and clichés, but they want to see religion achieve a better society to ensure that all human beings enjoy their human dignity. Religion in the eighties is under challenge, for young people are tired of the hypocrisy of some religious leaders and the apparent irrelevance of religious institutions.

Religious education was discussed and it was felt that more effective ways of teaching the young and preparing people for parenthood were needed. Muslim participants appreciated the policy of some churches, which have made provision for the religious instruction of Muslim children by Muslim teachers. It was hoped that Christian schools throughout the region could do likewise. It was also deemed desirable for Muslim institutions to reciprocate with similar facilities for Christian students. No children should be compelled or coerced to attend classes on any religion without their parents' consent.

Concerned Muslims and Christians should help to produce curricular materials for the use of the appropriate educational authorities in their own countries. These materials should emphasize the basic universal values of each religion which support the family as an institution. Muslims and Christians should be given a fair and adequate introduction to the beliefs and practices of their Christian and Muslim neighbours, as well as their compatriots of other faiths.

In answer to several queries about divorce, polygamy and women's rights, Muslims said that legal provision should be made to enforce the principles expressed explicitly or implicitly in the Qur'an and Sunnah. Participants noted a number of efforts to interpret the received tradition in the light of modern conditions.

Participants

Dr Carmen A. Abubakar
Institute of Islamic Studies
University of the Philippines
Diliman, Quezon City,
Philippines

Rev. Martin Adhikary
Baptist Mission, P.O. Box Bedgram
Dist. Gopalganj, Bangladesh

Adv. Moyeenud-Din Ahmed
81 Gagon Babu Road
Khulna, Bangladesh

Mr Syed A. Ali
Indian Institute of Islamic Studies
New Delhi 110 062, India

Mrs Naheed Ausaf Ali
Indian Institute of Islamic Studies

Rev. Dr S. Batumali
Seminari Theoloji Malaysia
Jalan Lima, Off Jalan Senturi
Kuala Lumpur 51000, Malaysia

Dr Sam V. Bhajjan
Henry Martyn Institute of Islamic
Studies, P.O. Box 153
Hyderabad 500 001, India

Dr Stuart E. Brown
World Council of Churches
P.O. Box 66
1211 Geneva, 20, Switzerland

Prof. D. Chellappa
Tamilnadu Theological Seminary
Arasaradi, Madurai 625 010, India

Mr Asghar Ali Engineer
Institute of Islamic Studies
Irene Cottage, 2nd Floor
4th Road, Santacruz (East)
Bombay 400 055, India

Rev. Hilario M. Gomez
Union Theological Seminary
P.O. Box 841
Manila, Philippines 2800

Dr Ihromi
Sekolah Tinngi Theologia
27 Jalan Proklamasi
Jakarta, Indonesia

Dr Habibur-Rahman Khan
World Conference on Religion and
Peace
240 Garden East
Karachi, Pakistan

Dr Inamullah Khan
World Muslim Congress
P.O. Box 5030
Karachi 3, Pakistan

Br Mohammed Ibrahim Khan
Fiji Muslim League
P.O. Box 3990 Samabula
Suva, Fiji

Mr Rahat Khan
Ittefaq Group of Publications Ltd
1 Ramkrishna Mission Road
Dhaka 3, Bangladesh

Dr Nurchalis Madjid
Jl. Johari I/8
Tanah Kusir
Jakarta 12240, Indonesia

Bishop I.W. Mastra
Jl. Debe 56, Denpasar,
Bali, Indonesia

Mr Yunus Mazni
Dewan Dakah Islamiyah
Jl. Cikini Raya 95, lt 5
Jakarta, Indonesia

Fr Eliseo R. Mercado
Missionary Oblates of Mary
Immaculate
29 Sampaguita Street
Cotabato City 9301, Philippines

Dr Hasan Qasim Murad
B-65, Block 4-A
Gulshan-i Iqbal
Karachi, Pakistan

Prof. Dr Mushirul Haq
Department of Islamic
and Arab-Iranian Studies
Jamia Millia Islamia
P.O. Jamianagar
New Delhi 110 025, India

Rt Rev. Dr S.A.E. Nababan
Kantor Pusat HKBP
Pearaja-Tarutung
Tapanuli-Utara, Indonesia

Rt Rev. Michael J. Nazir Ali
c/o Anglican Consultative Council
Floor 5, Partnership House
157 Waterloo Road
London, SE1 8UU, England

Dr M. Amin Rais
Jl. K.H.A. Dahlan 99
Jogyakarta, Indonesia

Mr Hamza Rusjdi
Panji-Masyarakat Magazine
Jl. Penjernihan 12A
Jakarta, Indonesia

Mr D. Santosa
Jl. Seno I 11
Jakarta Selatan 12510, Indonesia

General T.B. Simatupang
Jl. Deponegoro 55
Jakarta, Indonesia

Mrs Hetty Siregar
Kav. Pobri Kayumas V 331
Jakarta 13210, Indonesia

Rev. Dr Achilles de Souza
Archbishop's House
St Patrick's Cathedral
Karachi 3, Pakistan

Rev. Alfons Suhardi
Jl. Kramar Raya 134
Jakarta 10430, Indonesia

Mr Steven Sularto
Kompas (Daily)
Jl. Palmerah Selatan 26
Jakarta Selatan, Indonesia

Rev. Dr Victor I. Tanja
Majelis Sinode GPIB
Jl. Merdeka Timur 10
Jakarta, Indonesia

Dr Abdurrachman Wachid
Chairman of the Nahdatul-Ulama
Kramat Raya 164
Jakarta 10430, Indonesia

HJ. Fadlullah Wilmot
Regional Islamic Da'wah Council
of Southeast Asia and the Pacific
5th Floor, PERKIM Building
Jalan Ipoh, 51200 Kuala Lumpur
Malaysia

Rev. Akuila D. Yabaki
Methodist Church in Fiji
P.O. Box 357
Suva, Fiji

Mrs Sonja Toesoef
Jl. Bangha II M/3
Jakarta 12720, Indonesia

III. 3
Religion and Society

This meeting brought together Christians and Muslims from two regions, Europe and the Middle East. We met in the excellent setting of the Orthodox Academy of Crete, in Kolymbari beside the sea. After our opening on 27 September, we spent two days discussing each of two subjects: (a) the place of religious pluralism in today's social and political structures, and (b) the role of believers in promoting mutual trust and community. For each subject, we first heard a series of four preparatory talks, then spent a full day in group discussions. The talks were given in either English or French, with interpretation into the other, and there was one group for each of these two languages. Each morning began with a pair of brief devotional readings.

The distinguished co-chairmen of our colloquium were Dr Abdul Hakim Tabibi (vice-president of the Islamic Call Society Foundation, Geneva) and Mgr Georges Khodr (Greek Orthodox Metropolitan of Mount Lebanon). The participants represented a broad range of experience and viewpoints and the conversations were sincere, open and informative. Some forty years separated the eldest from the youngest and the presence and active participation of several women gave our deliberations a welcome dimension that is still much too rare in interfaith encounters. We are confident that everyone went home on 1 October with new insights and renewed commitment to the cause of inter-religious harmony, and we hope that this report will help others to reaffirm their own interest and efforts in the same cause.

RELIGIOUS PLURALISM: ANGLOPHONE GROUP

T. Ian Young

In our first session, we prepared the ground and attempted to define terms and concepts. Firstly, the group raised the question of the definition of religious pluralism:
— Where does it spring from?
— Is it revealed?
— Is it organized by the state?
For some, religious pluralism is a new experience, as in Western Europe where there is no set model, whereas in some parts of the Middle East a model already exists. Should we follow that model? One participant gave his own experience, where Muslims now living in Europe are divided on this question — some want a model based on Sharia, while others say Sharia is dated and returning to it is therefore undesirable. This raised the whole question of "how do we organize religious pluralism"?

If you take the Sharia model, the question of organization does not arise because Sharia is "on the top". If it is not, then the problem is political; so how does the state organize pluralism? Does it have a hierarchical structure? Various situations were discussed including Lebanon, France and Holland.

Another approach was suggested: we could consider the state and the problem of religion in society. But first perhaps we should consider the question of knowledge. Any state is based on a system of knowledge — based on principles — a religion is based on a system of knowledge which is taken without discussion. By calling this knowledge *belief* or *faith* we put it outside any critical approach. Belief has to be respected as knowledge and it is manipulated by individuals within the society according to the interests of each individual within his own group, so the knowledge cannot be given as such without a critical approach. It is assumed when we speak about Sharia and Christian doctrine that they are based on unquestioned beliefs when they are in fact absolutely questionable.

In interfaith dialogue we must begin as WE together, not as US and THEM. Someone observed that there is an intellectual famine; there seems to be no common thinking, so WE must come together, bringing no preconceived ideas.

The discussion then ranged over situations in various countries, leading us to the question of the "privatization" of religion, and whether this is desirable. The model of France was raised: the state is neutral and within it religious groups work out their own response to revelation. Sometimes, however, a person sees attacks on his own religion which are not really there. In Islam, there is a fear in some quarters of scholarly criticism and experimentation.

We also noted a gap between intellectuals and people in the street, and we had an extended discussion on the words *discrimination* and *classification*. It was suggested that it was possible and perhaps necessary to classify groups, but that this did not necessarily involve discrimination with all the negative overtones that this word conveys. The group had a valuable discussion of the Muslim "whole" — "umma", and this led us into the second session.

RELIGIOUS PLURALISM: FRANCOPHONE GROUP

Mustapha Matbouli

First, we defined the theme which we were to discuss: What are the problems encountered by a Muslim living in a Western, Christian country? What are the problems encountered by a Christian living in an Islamic country? How should Muslims behave towards Christians? How should Christians act with regard to Muslims?

Some participants insisted on the need to distinguish between custom and religion. The two are often confused, especially by Europeans, so that criticisms of Islam are really just comments on the comportment of Muslims who have come to work in Europe. Such Muslims often have a relatively limited cultural background and, instead of adopting a neutral Islam for living peacefully in Europe, they apply their values and customs; this way of living evokes a series of questions among the Europeans: Why do women have lower status than men? Why are men polygamous? etc. In fact, the Sharia encourages equality between men and women and sets drastic limitations on polygamy.

Others raised the problem of decision-making among Muslims: certain Muslims affirm that non-Muslims do not enjoy the same rights as Muslims. Others affirm the opposite, and who can solve this problem?

There are similar questions about freedom of worship which could be put to Muslim authorities.

Some felt that the nature of Muslim-Christian relations differs between Europe and the Middle East. In Europe, the relation between Christian and Muslim is cultural, but that is not the case in the Middle East because the two partners (Christian and Muslim) share the same culture, and this makes for differences of approach. In the Middle East, the status of Christian and Muslim sets limits on their communication. Besides, this communication is superficial and does not work in times of crisis, when there is a breakdown in communications caused by mistrust and fear. It is therefore necessary to work for a sincere dialogue based on mutual trust, and we must set this relationship on solid foundations which will assure stability in security.

A Christian noted the methodological risk inherent in any confusion of the two situations in which Christians and Muslims find themselves together, in Europe and the Middle East. This confusion must be rejected for three essential reasons:

1) a moral reason: as a Christian one refuses to identify with any given Western government, because one rejects any bargaining between Christians and any government, European or other, in order to apply pressure on Middle Eastern governments in the hope of guaranteeing the rights of Eastern Christians;
2) a political reason: every time the Christians have associated themselves with big power politics, they have lost;
3) a historical reason: Arab Christians are at home, whereas the Muslim living in Europe is not in his place of origin.

In this context, we can ask a double question: What is real Islam? What is real Christianity? According to one colleague, the answer is very simple: there is neither real Islam nor real Christianity because of the variety of interpretations of scripture.

Another Christian from the Middle East asked two further questions: Do the Muslims accept a civil society in which all citizens are equal? Why may Muslims ask European societies to apply their philosophy of human rights on their behalf, while Middle Eastern Christians do not have the same rights?

It was recalled that the two societies do not have the same conception of the state. In the Middle East, religion and politics overlap in all areas. The idea of state in the Middle East is vague and evasive. By contrast, in the West the boundaries between state and religion are well-defined. The separation of church and state in France (1905), for example, clearly spelled out the rules of the game. The French polity is neutral in its relationships with the religions of France. The religions have no right to interfere in affairs of state, and in return the state guarantees freedom of conscience and freedom of worship.

Thus, when a French Muslim claims freedom of conscience and freedom of worship, he makes his request as a citizen. Nevertheless such initiatives do not always succeed.

According to several participants, it has become imperative for us to undertake a pluridisciplinary reflection on the relation between state and religion(s) in the Middle East. Such a study would help us better understand this ambiguous relation which serves the purpose of religious and political power-brokers.

One colleague regretfully noted that the others had not taken sufficient account of the complexity of the situations we were examining: the situation of Muslims in Europe, the situation of Christians in the Middle East; the situation of European expatriates living in Islamic countries. Modernity, he said, leaves no place for plurality and he recalled the attitude which Mr Lamb had attributed to the majority of Britons: be like us or suffer the consequences. Secularism offers a limited plurality: in France the Muslims are offered only a supervised freedom of religion.

Another colleague stressed the importance of the New Muslim presence in Europe. This is greatly altering a whole set of social, political, religious and cultural data. We must struggle against racism, and for the respect of the rights, of the New Muslim communities, insisting on their share of all the freedoms provided by the state. Similarly, Muslims are called to collaborate with Christians in order to dissipate the tensions created in the Middle East by disrespect for the aspirations of Eastern Christians.

One final participant underlined the futility of denying the basic dissymmetry between the Christian and Islamic concepts of society and politics; these conceptions are the products of both theology and history, for the positions are not stable and uniform on either side. For example, freedom of conscience was imposed on the Christian churches and authorities. Then the churches accepted it and tried to justify the new situation. Even though the bases of justification were already there, they had not been used, for each religion has its own very strong self-censoring mechanisms. In Islamic countries, secularism was introduced by Western colonial authorities and was therefore highly suspect, as a foreign notion, in the minds of the Muslims. But the Muslims nevertheless kept certain elements: they want Western technology but not rational values and models. There is therefore a double standard. In the same way in politics, certain typically Western concepts have found their place; for example, democracy (for shura is really something quite different).

Religion currently functions as a norm for history, claiming that history has no influence over it. It is unfortunate that the two religions do not recognize what history has done to each of them. It is urgent for them both to be explained in the light of history without abandoning their normative role, for we still need a criterion of evaluation. Islam, like Christianity, grew from contradictory positions, struggles and quests for truth, a truth which can only be reached through a search that is sinuous and incomplete.

God's revelation is unique, noted this participant, but theologians have not contributed to a realization of unity between religions. One who obeys the Ten Commandments, one who applies the precepts of the Sermon on the Mount and one who follows the teachings of the Qur'an all contribute to understanding between believers.

Even the history of the revelation of the Qur'an *(nasikh, mansukh)* shows that God himself has a sense of history, that for God history is not something negligible, but that he seeks to introduce his word in the context of history. That suggests the possibility of new ways of reading the Qur'an, without claiming that they are absolute. This does not mean rejecting what God has revealed, but it points to a willingness to understand revelation in ways that take new circumstances and interests into account, because God himself has done so. That, says our colleague, would resolve a lot of problems.

TRUST AND COMMUNITY: ANGLOPHONE GROUP

Sultana Saeed

The following points and questions were raised and discussed in our group:
1. Who is a Mushrik?
2. How do you define Ummah to reach ijma'?
3. Why are Christians (i.e. the church) and the Muslims anxious to open this dialogue?

4. What part is played by the media in promoting or discouraging understanding?
5. Is there a problem of communication with the media... with each other?
6. Who is qualified to represent Islam?

Someone asked for clarification about: (1) the concept of Mushrikeen, and (2) how one defines the concept of Ummah to reach ijma'. The Muslims noted that throughout history these two concepts have been difficult to define, but a response was offered. Mushrikeen are people who believe in several gods, polytheists. They are distinguished from Ahl al-Kitab. The early Arabs were idol-worshippers and the message to them was to become Ahl al-Kitab, but they kept on refusing; the Ka'bah and their idols were sacred to them. So the Mushrikeens fought for what they thought was important.

We know there is tension in the world today and to lessen the tension we can take the discussion to another level and begin to understand the notion of "sacred". What was sacred to those people in the past? Indeed, what is sacred to the people of today — their materialism — their worldly goods? It is worth remembering that importance is not given to these sacred things by the intellectuals.

It is absolutely important that we come out of this polemical situation. The other alternative would be to go on to the theological level but if we do we will find that not only are important questions buried by theologians, but they present themselves as "humble", and "full of love"; yet either directly or indirectly they have contributed massively to the destruction of the cultures and identity of colonial peoples.

As for Ummah to reach ijma', ijma' is consensus; consensus of whom? The Ummah — but where does one find this? Now in the first five centuries of the Hijra, when Islam was going through its jurisprudential development, the 'ulama' perhaps agreed on who or what would be the Ummah. They could not have conceived the whole of the Muslim community to be the Ummah. On the physical level this would have been impossible; besides, we would have to get around the Shi'a-Sunni syndrome, e.g. the Shi'a did not recognize Sunni books and vice versa. The question has always been, how to put together the Ummahs of different parts of the Muslim world to reach ijma'. So the message is to *consult*.

How does one put this message on a pragmatic level? Consultation itself might only be an aspiration, a psychological need. Some say that ijma' can be the ijma' of a given generation. Ummah is an aspiration;

ijma' is the fourth source of Islamic law. This again is a theoretical concept. Here again we can adopt an anthropological approach; the practice of a given group, which in its turn is dependent on culture, language, traditions. In this model the group has something to relate to. In Islamic countries this has been done at different levels. In the Muslim world the oldest layer exists, the aspirations exist, but anthropologists are looking for it. If we conduct sociological research on the implementation of shari'a we will find that in some parts it is the customs of the people that were being applied. This is an approach to the problem to lessen tension.

Other participants observed that the theologians were respectful of local culture, or underlined that what matters is what the Qur'an says about the attitude to adopt. After Abraham the concepts of kufr and shirk came into play only when believers started coming into contact with non-believers of the time. Therefore Islam emphasized freedom of choice: accept Islam or reject Islam.

In the West, Ummah is seen as a threat because it magnifies the existence of people of alien culture, but it is in the nature of Islam to open up: take the example of India. It is also important to understand people's fear, anxiety and caution, so it is not a question of theology or anthropology, but one of perception. One needs Ummah, in order not to feel isolated, to have a kind of protective shield around one and to give a person a sense of belonging. It was also noted that the Qur'an does refer to "prophets" that are not mentioned, even in the Qur'an; the reference is in the nature of "one for every generation", *before* the seal of prophethood.

We had a further discussion on "opening up": is there a need to understand Islam or is there fear of communism or even atheism? Not necessarily "fear", because some atheists are just as concerned about social justice as we. It is not a question of uniting against anybody. Besides there is a belief that God very often works outside the churches. When freedom was stifled in the colonies, the churches protested against oppression. We can learn much from people outside (atheists, communists, etc.).

We have a number of churches adopting a ghetto mentality; there should be concern and struggle for opening up. The dialogue programme is very important but one of the least-funded ones.

There are extra-curricular reasons for opening. Are there also theological reasons that make people cross the boundaries and open up? Or have they some motive? A substantial number of people do move one way or the other for some reason. Is Islam regarded as a threat? If we are working for understanding, then we have to take this at its face value, we do not have to be convinced of *bonafide* reasons. If we have specific reasons for understanding, that is justification enough.

Converts sometimes make valuable contributions to the new community, and at times can adopt very rigid attitudes. The black Muslims of the USA do not stay within the Islamic framework, but create a different set-up by going beyond.

Who is qualified to share in ijma'? Inside Islam there is an ongoing debate on the status of Imam-e-mujtahid. It is important to distinguish within Islamic states as to who has authority. The Imam-e-mujtahid not only has to possess political power but he has to have the intellectual capacity. In all this one has to bear in mind the difference between Shi'is and Sunnis. In Pakistan the elected members of the legislative assembly have the right to be members of decision-making bodies but not all have religious knowledge. The Pakistan government has appointed others to advise members of the Assembly. This was cited to indicate one way to achieve ijma'. There is a danger that this situation may disintegrate into party politics and pressure group operations. At times the issue is not purely religious, but an issue of power. Other examples were cited but participants agreed that it was important to remember that ijma' means giving a chance to all. But one cannot have on the same level a university professor and a labourer, and there is a question amongst the Mujtahideen in Afghanistan as to who should be elected. This is very similar to the situation in previous centuries, when the question posed was whether Uthman or someone else should be elected. This problem of whom to elect has to be faced.

We can help those with whom we work towards a better understanding through dialogue, where a convergence of thoughts takes place; this is a spiritual activity, a spiritual venture. It is a subconscious decision; each person is different. This could be done on a human level, e.g. in the education of children.

There are two types or groups of Christians: those who share the gospel or try to reach out and meet Muslims, and other who are more withdrawn, more afraid. Even so dialogue is more possible on a day-to-day human level rather than on a theological plane, which can be intimidating. People involved in helping others are also, whilst reaching out, involved in a learning process. Other people are so occupied with their own things that they do not wish to trust or understand. It takes time to draw people out. "Love they neighbour" is a Christian message, but who is your neighbour? Find out for yourself. The person is there so you have to take the initiative.

In Lebanon and Egypt the scope in which interaction can take place is shrinking because people see their situation as precarious. We must first create a space for relating to each other, then other levels will follow. In Egypt, the church took the initiative in improving buildings and facilities, and Muslims followed suit. Trust develops as a result of initiative taken and does not grow by itself.

Minorities in Europe are suffering a great deal because all Muslims are lumped together. When one publishes a book, not a word appears in any of the papers, and yet when "radical Islam" appeared the media went out of their way to give extensive coverage. It is better not to approach the problem from a religious point of view, but look to Muslims as people having their own problems. Progress would be made if we got away from religious terminology. We need to change the vocabulary and look at the whole question from a cultural point of view. In Lebanon no one speaks of religious war, whereas in Europe this fight has become a religious war. There are also other difficulties, e.g. economic. The problem with Western media is that they put all the Muslims into one basket; e.g. on French TV during peak hour pictures have appeared showing a priest covered in blood, killed by a Muslim.

The presentation of Islam outside Muslim countries is a serious problem. Perhaps Muslims can learn from other minorities like the Poles or Greeks in the USA, or other minorities in Europe.

TRUST AND COMMUNITY: FRANCOPHONE GROUP

Constantin Patelos

At the outset, we observed that Muslims, Jews and Christians have a common life. These communities continue to exist under the eye of God for we live together and we receive together our "conviviality", a term of recent coinage that nevertheless bears very strong significance, far surpassing the idea of coexistence. In the space of this very "conviviality" or living together, even an ambivalent and equivocal term like toleration can be used if we adjust its contours: to have the patience of the just who can be in disagreement with their brothers but whose love for them is undiminished. The great toleration is to be indulgent with one's fellow monotheist. The Christian's task is to assimilate this word and give it a new doctrinal and spiritual content. Too often this spiritual dimension is quite forgotten in Muslim-Christian relations, but it is a dimension which would unite us in our differences and give meaning both to dialogue and interfaith collaboration. On this point, two clarifications emerged from the discussion.

Islam considers and commends the other as a human being with rights to life and a fair share. Christian reflection is not guided by juridical principles; it is not a question of law but of heart. We must nevertheless be careful not to become overly schematic; we should also keep in mind the plural character of any religion. If we stay only on the plane of law, we run the risk of reducing Islam to the level of a school. There are of course suras which regulate relations between Muslims and people of other faiths, but there is much more. We must understand the spirit of Islamic law in its profundity, although it has generally been taken in a spirit of positivist law, yet unexhausted. The Arabic language, which frames these laws, is the language of individuals filled with their own spirit and emotions. A semantic effort is needed, going to the roots. This requirement can be traced to the very beginnings of the Islamic state and *fiqh*, the cornerstones of the edifice of Islamic society. This work has been reductionist, transforming a spiritual law into a law of calculations. By returning to the spirit of the Qur'an, and not that of the *fuquha'*, we can understand the fullness of the Qur'anic laws in their spiritual dimension. The example of the mystics was cited, for they defied the jurisconsults and sought Islam beyond the laws.

This type of dialogue demands that each partner should be aware of the ambiguities in the terms, for their experiences are not identical. Can such dialogue occur without a doctrinal debate? Can we say that the doctrinal debate is not necessary here, because this dialogue deals with social questions? To promote this dialogue we must further note that the partners are present with all their heart and no feelings of power. We do not come to impose or coerce or convert anyone to another's faith. We must speak honestly and avoid banalities. We should reflect on where we go from here and not just wait for the end of time.

To tell the truth, it was not Western Christianity which urged people to claim their freedom, said a few participants, but European liberalism. A person may proclaim his faith without forcing the other to change. In Islam, *da'wah* is an obligation, it is part of a Muslim's commitment. The

Qur'an mentions it clearly, urging Muslims to call others to follow the path of God. As a condition, the Qur'an requires sincerity and as a risk it recognizes dialogue of the best sort, infused with wisdom.

Let us deepen our own faith and practise it, bringing ourselves nearer to our neighbours for the good of humanity.

We also talked about the content of dialogue. There is ritual dialogue, where everyone speaks politely but says little. There are people who bring their personal agenda to the meetings. In order to understand one another well, we need a certain acquaintance with one another, but most of all we need to go beyond this acquaintance and speak frankly and openly, of course without abandoning our good manners.

The future of Islam will affect all Christian communities in Europe and the Near East, and obviously all the Muslim countries. What is this future? Where are human societies going and what role will faith have? Such questions can only be discussed in a spirit of mutual trust.

This trust needs buttresses. We must eliminate those forms of violence (verbal and military) which are found everywhere, especially on the backs of the Christians living in the Near East and the Muslims settled in Western Europe. Among these forms of violence we must note the propaganda on television: France, Egypt, Federal Republic of Germany and Saudi Arabia were mentioned but the group did not wish to designate any "culprits". Even in university circles European Christians and Oriental Muslims are too often very ignorant of the basic beliefs of the other, and even denigrate the aspirations of the minorities in their own societies.

Action must begin with us. We must learn to use the opportunities and possibilities which appear, in order to support the rights of Muslim communities in Western Europe and to promote the rights of all citizens, Christian and Muslim, in the countries of the Near East. We must watch over the images of our partners presented by the media in our own countries. It behoves us to cast a critical glance on the training of our spiritual leaders. Finally, we ought always to keep a sense of balance in considering differing situations. When we refer to the complaints of the Christian communities in the Near East, we should bear in mind the grievances of the Muslims in Western Europe, and vice versa. And it is our duty to decry loudly the abuses of the other which our own communities may perpetrate. Together we can build societies where every person will feel truly free to serve God according to his or her own conscience.

Participants

Dr Syed Z. Abedin
P.O. Box 8856
Jeddah, Saudi Arabia

Dr Mohamed Arkoun
44 Bld de Magenta
75010 Paris, France

Mrs Marie B. Assaad
1095 Corniche El Nil
Garden City, Cairo, Egypt

Pasteur Jean-Claude Basset
Concorde 15
1203 Geneva, Switzerland

Dr Ahmad Baydoun
c/o Dr Tarek Mitri
P.O. Box 4259
Limassol, Cyprus

Mr Souhib Bencheikh El Hocine
Institut musulman
de la Mosquée de Paris
Place du Puits l'Ermite
75005 Paris, France

Dr Mahmoud Bouzouzou
Rte de Loëx 5 ter
1213 Onex, Switzerland

Dr Stuart E. Brown
World Council of Churches
P.O. Box 66
1211 Geneva 20, Switzerland

Dr Samia Chaar
c/o Mr Sami Chatilu
P.O. Box 1458
Beirut, Lebanon

Mrs Valerie Fisher
All Hallows School
Ditchingham, Bungay
Suffolk NR35 2DU, England

Fr Michael Fitzgerald
Secretariat for Non-Christians
00120 Vatican City, Italy

Dr Juliette Haddad
BP 113-5687
Beirut, Lebanon

Mr M. Saleh Hamid
WCRP, 14 rue Auguste Vilbert
1218 Grand Saconnex, Switzerland

Metropolitan Georges Khodr
Broummana, Lebanon

Rev. Dr Christopher Lamb
Coventry Cathedral
7 Priory Row
Coventry, CV1 5ES, England

Dr Mustapha Matbouli
6 rue Sainte Catherine
67000 Strasbourg, France

Dr Jemaa Messaoudi
105 rue de Theux
1040 Brussels, Belgium

Dr Tarek Mitri
P.O. Box 4259
Limassol, Cyprus

Dr Constantin G. Patelos
Terpsithéas 26
17563 Paleon Phaliron, Greece

Dr S. Saeed
Flat 68, 6 Hall Road
London NW8 9PB, England

Dr Ghassan Salame
9 avenue Victor Hugo
75016 Paris, France

Rev. Jan Slomp
Postbus 203
3830 AE Leusden, Netherlands

Dr Abdul Hakim Tabibi
81 rue de Lyon
1203 Geneva, Switzerland

Père Christian Van Nispen
c/o Collège de la Sainte Famille
B.P. 73 Faggalah
Cairo, Egypt

Père Hans Vocking
Postfach 170427
6000 Frankfurt 17
Federal Republic of Germany

Rev. Ian Young
P.O. Box 36
Manama, Bahrain, Arabian Gulf

III. 4

The Challenge of Pluralism

The fourth regional colloquium brought people from several parts of the USA and Canada to the New Windsor Service Center in rural Maryland from 17 to 21 March 1988. Dr Fuad Sahin (president of the Canadian Muslim Association) and Rev. Clark Lobenstine (executive director ot the Interfaith Conference of Metropolitan Washington) served ably as our co-chairpersons, and our diligent and perceptive rapporteurs were Dr David Kerr and Mr Imtiyaz Yusuf. Each morning we heard two addresses on the day's theme. Our three themes were: religion and family, religion and economics, and religion and education.

About a third of our number were women, which is quite a healthy segment for meetings of this type and offers hope for an even better ratio in future gatherings. The broad range of age, experience, professional background and geographic residence enriched the discussions with a variety of contributions, sometimes blending into a spontaneous consensus and at other times opening a full gamut of perspectives and options for further reflection. It is our earnest hope that this report will sustain this reflection among us and encourage others to consider seriously the issues which it raises and engage in constructive interfaith encounters whenever the occasion arises.

RELIGION AND FAMILY

DAVID KERR

John Borelli's presentation focused upon two realities relevant to our discussion of family life in North America: the demise of traditional patterns of family and matrimony, and the continuingly high evaluation laid upon family life, in varying forms, among the majority of North Americans. He left us with the challenge: the need to reaffirm the values which our religions place upon marriage, but with this the need to address ourselves pastorally to the reality of the radically changing social situation of family life in North America.

Riffat Hassan did not accept to begin with North America as the context of her discussion of the experience of women in Muslim society and family life. Why, she asked, should Western Christian experience set the framework, agenda and questions for dialogue. She shared her experience of the personal cost, as a woman, of the struggle to achieve justice for her personhood in a Muslim society (Pakistan), and went on to explain how this isolation was intensified in her life in North America. The struggle for justice, she testified, demands suffering and personal sacrifice.

From these points of departure, in addition to the earlier presentations of Mahmoud Ayoub and Byron Haines, our discussion ranged over the following five broad issues.

How do we see our ethical responsibility as religious communities in this situation? Some felt strongly that church and mosque should resist the decline of traditional values by reaffirming religious teaching compassionately yet correctively. (Too often have church and mosque been more inclined to accommodate than to guide, in the view of some participants.) Others emphasized that church and mosque must accept responsibility for many of the oppressive aspects of family life which, through the patriarchal forms of our respective religions, inflict the lives of women and young people in particular. These de-personalizing facts of male domination must be reformed if we are to deal honestly with the situations of human alienation and isolation which exist so widely throughout North American societies.

We discussed, with difficulty and inconclusively, what we may have to learn of the guidance and correction of God's will as it can be discerned in the experience of the oppressed, the socially-marginalized, and those who live in exceptional styles of family life: for example, homosexuals. The alternative models of family life which are increasingly experimented in North America demand our self-critical attention and theological reflection, so that such comparison as is properly to be made between them and the traditional values of our religions may be freed of complacency and judgmental hypocrisy. Mercy, we agreed, is a fundamental and ethically-creative element of our two religions.

A similar variety of questions surfaced around the involvement of our religions in the professedly secular societies of North America, and our attitudes towards secularism. Is it either honest or effective, we asked, to pass *generalized* condemnation on secular society as something alien to the understanding of community in church and mosque? On the other hand, is it sufficient to express only misgiving with the civil religion of "Americanism"? Whether or not it is by choice that we live in North American societies, we recognize that they do offer us certain benefits: for example, the freedom to practise a diversity of religious and social forms in a pluralist social context; and the freedom to think and act critically, including the freedom to criticize society itself; the value of the person which enables women to claim justice. North American models of secular pluralism are not necessarily the best, far less the only models we should consider. India, Tanzania, Britain, for example, represent alternatives which we mentioned though without time to discuss them. Dialogue with peoples in these situations can mature and sharpen our proper criticism of North American societies and help us evolve creative alternatives to the status quo.

We affirmed that our faith perspective on these issues starts from the acclamation of both the Bible and Qur'an that God's will is sovereign. As Muslims and Christians we share a determination to be instruments of God's will in the places where we live, and by God's grace this may preserve us from the *pessimism* which a statistical analysis of family life in North America could induce. Our ultimate failure would be to do nothing.

But we agreed that faith is not a licence for triumphalism; it does not side-step the task of analysis; it is tested and testified in what we do; and it impels us to relate pastorally to our neighbours as they and we are. The companion of faith is realism, and our religious alternative to the status quo must be viable and possible of realization. Reversion to a "Christian society" or the creation of an "Islamic state" in North America are equally inconceivable because neither is practicable, were we to agree that either was desirable — which we did not. We did agree that the challenge of church and mosque to the status quo in North American societies is made by the persuasive power of *example*, not the attempt to coerce, which was neither biblical nor qur'anic.

While these generalities were agreed, we shared some difference of opinion about the *modalities* of the ethical task of church and mosque in addressing this situation. Some wished to accentuate the duty of correcting current practices of family life which diverge from the values of our religious sources in scripture and Tradition. Our consciousness of the *continually reformist* duty of church and mosque was here identified with the responsibility to reaffirm normative rules in biblical and qur'anic moral teaching which are fundamental to a religious way of life. The qur'anic imperative to "command what is approved and forbid the indecent" is in harmony with the biblical Decalogue (Ten Commandments). This duty was perceived as one of mercy, not judgment which is the prerogative of God alone, and it finds its legitimacy in what God has decreed to be the divine will.

Respectful of this view, others wished to emphasize the imperative of being open to discern God's will in history and in evolving patterns of human behaviour which, even in divergence from particular scriptural regulations, may embody positive principles of human relationships of which scripture approves. Here we expressed our consciousness of the *continual reformation* needed within our religious communities as part of the renewal of society. We felt the need to be surprised by new perceptions of God's will in forms of human relationships which our religious traditions may not have sufficiently understood. The question of how to discern and assess what is of God's will in our histories and contemporary situations remained before us as a critical though unresolved question.

In Islamic terms we discussed the issue of *ijtihad*, which we could paraphrase as "striving to discern and apply God's will in our societies". For some *ijtihad* was seen as something we are all doing in many different ways, intellectually and practically. But are there limits to *ijtihad*, others asked, and if so how are they defined? We could explain *ijtihad* as a juristic mechanism, but the question of how to exercise it in the secular pluralism of North American societies calls for more discussion. It was recalled that more than half a century ago, Muhammad Iqbal defined *ijtihad* as "the principle of movement in Islam", and the wider terms as the process of change which all religions need if they are to remain dynamic forces for the moral-spiritual transformation of society.

It was in this perspective that we discussed the question of family life. Clearly the family is a *central* inspiration of both Christianity and Islam. But it is perhaps the Roman Catholic identification of matrimony as a sacrament, more than the Protestant concept of a human contract in the sight of God, which distinguishes Christian and Muslim views of marriage and therefore of the value of the family. Without denigrating the family, some cautioned against the danger of overloading its value, for fear of making idolatry of virtue and prejudging other forms of human relationships as inviable and immoral.

The extended family was seen to have certain social benefits beyond those of the nuclear family, but we questioned whether traditional forms of the extended family, belonging to agrarian societies, were viable in the mobile societies of the industrialized world. This challenged us to ask whether our local communities could not operate more effectively in the role of extended families.

Interfaith marriages were (too briefly) discussed in terms both of the unique opportunity they provide for faith traditions to meet in the intricate depths of human life, but also in terms of the social difficulties which partners encounter; and we were urged to avoid subjecting such marriages to harmful categorization.

Questions of our response to other forms of family life — single parenting, blended families, polygamous marriages, stable homosexual partnerships — were raised but insufficiently discussed for any consensus to emerge. Some Muslims as well as Christians wished to consider celibacy as a way of life for lay women and men, and the name of Rabi'a al-Adawiyyah, the woman mystic and poet of early Islam, was held up as an example of celibate piety. Islamic legal tradition mentions a number of human characteristics in relation to marriage; in this tradition a person who is not suited to be married should not marry.

RELIGION AND ECONOMICS

David Kerr

The presentations of Sulayman Nyang and Michael Cooke were striking in their fundamental agreement that striving for a just economic order is an essential religious duty of both Islam and Christianity; for Muslims it is part of the right practice of *zakat* (one of the five pillars — *arkan* — of

Islam) while for Christians it is has a *status confessionis* (i.e., it is part of the faith). During our discussions, much appreciation was expressed to the presenters.

As we sought clarifications from the presenters we were further struck by the convergence of biblical and qur'anic perspectives on the place of economics within the broad parameters of our belief systems. The unity of the creation and the wholeness of the earth within the providence of God *(tawhid)*; the sovereignty of God's lordship over the resources of the earth and their disposition within human history, the trust *(amanah)* which God has invested in humankind in giving us dominion or trustee-ship *(khilafah)*; the human responsibility for the just ordering of human society in harmony with the natural order of creation *(tazkiyah)*; and the inter-relatedness of this world with the further dimension of existence within God's sovereignty which we speak of as the after-life *(al-akhirah)*.

In further discussion we learned more about the latitude of contemporary Muslim interpretation of *zakat*, *riba* (usurious interest), *mudarabah* (profit and loss sharing) and *musharakah* (partnership). There was insufficient time to pursue Christian equivalents as developed by medieval theologians (e.g. Aquinas, Luther, Calvin) or by some modern documents, though it was recognized that such are fewer in number today than are the Muslim religious economic thinkers. Both traditions are concerned with just economic practice; some Christians mentioned the example of liberation theology. Muslims noted that the idea of a class struggle is foreign to Islam, and people from both traditions rejected consumerism and waste. A need was expressed for further examination of these issues on the Muslim side. As well, there was a call for deeper Christian research as a necessary task in the preparation of further Christian-Muslim dialogue on religion and economics.

We were strongly aware of the gap between our scriptural principles and the reality of the societies in which we live. We confessed that the difference which confronts us is not a distance to be explained historically or sociologically, but a spiritual-ethical contradiction which places us directly under the judgment of God. In our present world it is not merely a matter of governments turning a deaf ear to ethical imperatives. By the standard of our scriptures it is an issue in which there can be neither mitigating circumstances nor neutrality. To fail to strive for justice in the economy is to connive in and perpetuate evil in the collective sense of social sin. In the US this is evidenced by the fact that 20 percent of the population has only 0.2 percent of the wealth, while another 20 percent has 70 percent of the wealth. To understand these disparities requires the analysis of multinational companies whose power exceeds that of national governments, and whose economic gain brings whole nations into oppressive crises of international debt. Muslims identified the multinationals with what the Qur'an names as *taghut* (idolatrous excess).

Muslims and Christians were unanimous that this situation urgently demands our repentance *(tawbah: metanoia)*, and return to the radical discipleship of scriptural standard. Jesus Christ began his teaching by quoting the prophet Isaiah: "The spirit of the Lord is upon me because He has anointed me to preach the Gospel to the poor...." (Luke 4:18). One of the earliest revelations to the prophet Muhammed commanded him: "O thou enveloped in thy cloak, arise and warn! Thy Lord magnify, thy raiment purify, pollution shun; and show not favour, seeking worldly gain!" (Q74:1-6). Repentance in the Bible and the Qur'an demands the radical moral reorientation of our lives as persons and communities, and as we discussed these perspectives together, we felt ourselves compelled by a sense of moral urgency.

The urgency of the crisis was underscored by our recognition that human abuse of the natural resources of the earth is part of our economic disorder. We are drawing on account from a finite reserve which is close to exhaustion. Our destruction of the ecosystem is at the point of no return. We hope that justice for the earth is recognized as the inalienable foundation of a just economic system.

What can we do? This became the burning question in our discussion. We cannot do nothing, though many of us felt paralyzed by the ambiguities of the realities of our lives. In a thousand ways we recognized that each of us is influenced directly and indirectly by the institutional forces of economic injustice, simply by living in North American societies. How do we make real our religious preferences for justice for the poor in our societies of wealth? Can we bite the hand that feeds us? How do we begin to confront the monumental institutions of socialized injustice which surround us?

Not to be overwhelmed by such problems, we agreed that repentance in both our scriptures demands a change of personal life-style as a beginning. Here we were helped by the articulation of three guidelines for action: (1) to deepen and extend the sense of moral urgency we must ground our changes of life-style within our local communities, (2) we must strive to effect change by identifying and exploiting such social power as we have, (3) we must develop creative experiments which keep our hope alive.

In conclusion of this day's discussion we felt united in the strong conviction that we must continue our dialogue in an imaginative process of deepening, building and action through which we can strive to effect change within our respective religious communities. We committed ourselves to plan for further action-oriented dialogue meetings which will disseminate our zeal through wider sections of our religious communities.

RELIGION AND EDUCATION

Imtiyaz Yusuf

Jane Smith, in her paper about approaches to the teaching of Islam in Christian theological institutions, raised a number of issues faced by both the teachers and the students. These ranged from topics relating to theology, social experience, religious values and the pluralistic nature of the world in which we live today. Jane also outlined the current trends in the study of Islam as (a) the interpreting of the other's religion (in this case Islam) as a heresy, (b) the trend that seeks reconciliation yet asserts the supremacy of one's own faith, (c) a third approach, according to which each religion being different in its vision of reality is to be recognized as simply different. Such an approach may lead to the affirmation of the "other" and help in mutual understanding, enabling both to understand the deep sense of related-ness among human beings.

Aziz Khaki in his treatment of "Islam and Education" referred to the history and philosophy of Muslim education, and talked of the notion of unity of knowledge and its treatment in the thought of Muslim scholars like Ibn Sina, al-Ghazzali, Ibn Rushd and Ibn Khaldun.

Moving on to the pluralistic situation of today which Muslims have come to know in North America, Aziz showed through examples how the interfaith situation in North America has led to changes in school curricula, especially in Canada. The question remains: How can we socialize younger generations as the values of our society become inter-religious?

The discussions that took place on these two papers may be arranged under two topics:
a) the issue of a public education system and the values of a religiously pluralistic society;

b) the issue of whether one has to be a declared Muslim or Christian to teach either tradition: in other words, the role of insider/outsider and the teaching of religion, in this case Islam or Christianity.

Discussions on topic (a) showed a shared concern on the part of both Muslims and Christians that religion should be given an appropriate place in the national educational system, for no discipline can be taught without an appreciation of the influence of religion, for no education is value-free. The Christians and Muslims together felt that their religious identification and values need to be reflected in the educating of youth. This will lead to an enriching of our experience and an understanding of each other in a plural society. Yet the issue of secular education and opposition to prayer in school (which has become politicized) did not go undebated. Some participants from both communities said they would prefer not to include prayer in the educational system, for the reasons we have already mentioned.

On the second topic (insider/outsider and teaching of religion), it was commonly felt that since religion is a common human experience, it is possible to experience religion on both fronts and gain insight into each other's tradition. In some ways we are all insiders/outsiders living in inter-relationship.

The Muslims strongly affirmed that it is often only an insider who can give a fully accurate account of his/her religious experience and tradition in an educational system. Whether such a demand is legitimate in today's state-education systems was also raised.

A Christian participant pointing to the reality of the contemporary plural situation indicated that the outsider/insider issue offers an opportunity to enrich ourselves by enabling us to talk about religion as life.

A Muslim said that if religion is taught in schools it should be taught as any other human science, with objectivity.

An interesting aspect of this session was that Muslims and Christians were divided into groups not according to religious identitites, but differences of opinion about which values need to be taught in schools: merely "morals" or morals based on religion.

An important part of this session was the lively dialogue between the Muslims and Christians on the question of sources of the Muslims' knowledge of Christianity in terms of history and theology. A Muslim participant said that the Muslims need to know more about Christ and Christianity, for Islam challenges the Muslims to reflect upon these themes as mentioned in Qur'an 5:3 and 5:69, verses which challenge the Muslims to accept plurality.

A Christian participant said that the issues of the Trinity and the Muslim view of Jesus are long-term problems worthy of reflection. At present many Christians are prepared to accept Muhammed as a prophet in some sense. There is still a question as to what Muslims think about Jesus.

A Christian presented a Christian view of God, and explained the doctrine of the Trinity. He said that Muslim and Christian concepts of God derived from our understandings of revelation. Christians know God as the father of the Lord Jesus Christ; that is to say, Christ was the fullest and more perfect showing of what God is. God is love and in Christ that love was fully revealed. God is compassionate and merciful and God's compassion and mercy met with humanity's sinful status in the death and resurrection of Jesus Christ. Since God is love, God suffers and the cross of Jesus Christ is the fullest expression of that suffering love, which embraced humanity and reconciled it to Godself.

In the case of the Trinity, therefore, the oneness of God is not simply mathematical, but a rich and living oneness. God is a full community, self-sufficient within Godself, so that doctrine of the Trinity is basically an expression of community within the Godhead.

Continuing on this topic, another Christian said that the first task in dialogue is mutual understanding: for Christians to explain Islam accurately and objectively in a manner that will be recognized by Muslims as essentially correct, and for Muslims to do the same in regard to Christianity. This is essentially a *historical* approach — understanding "history" as "the story" of that which is being explained, including the present as well as the past, and including the understanding of religions as involving real, living people. The *theological* questions of what Muhammed means to Christians, and Jesus to Muslims must also be faced, but as it is unlikely that definitive answers will be found in the near future — if ever — the *historical* approach must not wait for the theological.

Finally, another Christian wished to question both Muslims and Christians as to the meaning of the word "finality" in relation to prophethood. Only God is final. Christians have to struggle with the question of how God's will continued to be revealed after the time of Jesus Christ. This is a historical question, which requires us to take history seriously in theological perspective. Muhammed, the prophet most loved by Muslims and the one who inspired them to create a great religion and civilization, demands serious Christian theological evaluation.

The Muslims also have to deal with the personality of Jesus as representing love; the issue is not one of getting even but one for further dialogue and reflection.

Although this discussion did not resolve the issue, it did show how monotheism can serve as a basis for dialogue.

Participants

Dr Ann B. Alkadhi
9911 Vogue Lane
Houston, TX 77080, USA

Dr Mahmoud Ayoub
Canadian Institute for Advanced
Islamic Research
1183 Ossington Avenue
Canada, M6G 3W4

Dr Newell S. Booth, Jr
Department of Religion
Miami University
The Old Manse
Oxford, OH 45056, USA

Dr John Borelli
BCEIA/NCCB
1213 Massachusetts Avenue
Washington, DC 20005-4105, USA

Dr Stuart E. Brown
Sub-unit on Dialogue
World Council of Churches
P.O. Box 66
1211 Geneva 20, Switzerland

Mr Michael Cooke
The Ecumenical Forum of Canada
11 Madison Avenue
Toronto, Canada M5R 2S2

Mrs Nabila Drooby
1528 Harold
Houston, TX 77006, USA

Rev. Canon S.A. Farah
129 Church Avenue
Willowdale
Ontario, Canada M2N 4G3

Sr Donna Geernaert
Canadian Conference of Catholic
Bishops
90 Parent Avenue
Ottawa, Canada K1N 7B1

Mr William G. Gepford
Littlefield Presbyterian Church
7560 Littlefield Blvd.
Dearborn, MI 48126, USA

Dr Byron Haines
OCMR/NCCCUSA
77 Sherman Street
Hartford, CT 06105, USA

Dr Riffat Hassan
774 David Fairleigh Ct., Apt.3
Louisville, KY 40217, USA

Dr David A. Kerr
Hartford Seminary
77 Sherman Street
Hartford, CT 06105, USA

Mr Aziz Khaki
701 Millyard
Vancouver, Canada V5Z 3Z9

Rev. Clark Lobenstine
Interfaith Conference
1419 V Street N.W.
Washington, DC 20009-55806, USA

Rev. Elizabeth Marmura
St Luke's United Church
353 Sherbourne Street
Toronto, Canada M5A 2S3

Dr S. Moizul Matin
37 Pardee Circle
Princeton, NJ 08540, USA

Dr Mohammad Mehdi
National Council on Islamic Affairs
P.O. Box 416
New York, NY 10017, USA

Dr Sulayman S. Nyang
African Studies and Research
Howard University
Washington, DC 20059, USA

Dr Fathi Osman
Islamic Center for Southern California
434 South Vermont
Los Angeles, CA 90020, USA

Dr A. Fuad Sahin
RR No. 1
Niagara-on-the-Lake
Ontario, Canada LO5 1JO

Dr Jane I. Smith
Iliff School of Theology
2201 South University Blvd
Denver, CO 80210, USA

Ms Suna Umari
The Rothko Chapel
1409 Sul Ross
Houston, TX 77006, USA

Mr Imtiyaz Yusuf
120-1300 Columbia Avenue
Philadelphia, PA 19122, USA